Praise for
Mark Batterson

"With *Soulprint*, Mark Batterson has done it again! He has asked the questions that led me into a self-discovery that enlarged my vision of God's purpose in my life."

—RUTH GRAHAM, speaker and author of *Fear Not Tomorrow, God Is Already There*

"As a leader and teacher, Mark Batterson brings imagination, energy, and insight. Mark's genuine warmth and sincerity spill over into his communication, combining an intense love for his community with a passionate desire to see them living the life God dreams for them. I appreciate his willingness to take bold risks and go to extraordinary lengths to reach our culture with a message that is truly relevant."

—ED YOUNG, senior pastor of Fellowship Church

"A thoughtful and energetic leader, Mark Batterson presses us to consider how we live out our faith in the world around us. When Mark has something to say, I am quick to listen."

—FRANK WRIGHT, PhD, president and CEO of National Religious Broadcasters

"Too many of us are doing life at an unsustainable pace and losing sight of our first love. In *Primal*, Mark Batterson invites you to rediscover the reality of Christ and His passions. This book will challenge you, push you, and stretch you. You will walk away righteously aggravated, but catapulted into action."

—CRAIG GROESCHEL, senior pastor of LifeChurch.tv; author of *Chazown, Dare to Drop the Pose,* and *Love, Sex & Happily Ever After*

"In *Primal,* Mark weaves us through the Great Commandment with insights that are both winsome and wise, piquing both curiosity and conviction. He calls us to a discipleship free of the trappings of shriveled self-concern, drawing us to give ourselves, with abandon, to others as we heed Jesus' call to 'love God' above all."

—GARY HAUGEN, president and CEO of International Justice Mission and author of *Good News About Injustice, Terrify No More,* and *Just Courage*

"Mark, I'm with you. It's time for the believers to be more. Let's hear the voice of God and be that holy passionate fire that we are called to be. It's the primal way."

—SHAUN ALEXANDER, 2005 NFL MVP, acclaimed speaker and author of *Touchdown Alexander* and *The Walk*

mark batterson

SOUL PRINT

discovering your divine destiny

MULTNOMAH
BOOKS

SOULPRINT
PUBLISHED BY MULTNOMAH BOOKS
12265 Oracle Boulevard, Suite 200
Colorado Springs, Colorado 80921

The names of some individuals whose stories are told in this book have been changed to
protect their privacy.

ISBN 978-1-60142-039-8
ISBN 978-1-60142-334-4 (electronic)

Cover design by Mark Ford

Published in association with Eames Literary Services, Nashville, Tennessee.

Published in the United States by WaterBrook Multnomah, an imprint of the Crown
Publishing Group, a division of Random House Inc., New York.

MULTNOMAH and its mountain colophon are registered trademarks of Random House Inc.

Library of Congress Cataloging-in-Publication Data
Batterson, Mark.
    Soulprint : discovering your divine design / Mark Batterson. — 1st ed.
        p. cm.
    ISBN 978-1-60142-039-8 — ISBN 978-1-60142-334-4 (electronic)
1. Self-realization—Religious aspects—Christianity. 2. Young adults—Religious life.
3. Christian life. I. Title.
    BV4529.2.B38 2011
    248.8'4—dc22
                                            2010041765

Printed in the United States of America
2012

10 9 8 7 6 5 4 3 2

SPECIAL SALES
Most WaterBrook Multnomah books are available at special quantity discounts when
purchased in bulk by corporations, organizations, and special interest groups. Custom
imprinting or excerpting can also be done to fit special needs. For information, please
e-mail SpecialMarkets@WaterBrookMultnomah.com or call 1-800-603-7051.

To Mom and Dad…
You helped me discover my soulprint.

Contents

OPENING

Soulprint

The dullest and most uninteresting person
you can talk to may one day be a creature
which, if you saw it now, you would be
strongly tempted to worship.... It is in the
light of these overwhelming possibilities…
that we should conduct all our dealings
with one another, all friendships, all loves,
all play, all politics. There are no *ordinary*
people. You have never talked to a mere
mortal.

—C. S. LEWIS, *The Weight of Glory*

There has never been and never will be anyone else like you. But that isn't a testament to you. It's a testament to the God who created you. You are unlike anyone who has ever lived. But that uniqueness isn't a virtue. It's a responsibility. Uniqueness is God's gift to you, and uniqueness is your gift to God. You owe it to yourself to *be yourself.* But more important, you owe it to the One who designed you and destined you.

Make no mistake, this is no self-help book. Self-help is nothing more than idolatry dressed up in a rented tuxedo. So let me be blunt: you aren't good enough or gifted enough to get where God wants you to go. Not without His help. But here's the good news: there is nothing God cannot do in you and through you if you simply yield your life to Him. All of it. All of you.

This book is all about you, but it's not about you at all. The fact that there never has been and never will be anyone like you simply means that no one can worship God like you or for you. *You were created to worship God in a way that no one else can.* How? By living a life no one else can—your life. You have a unique destiny to fulfill, and no one can take your place. You play an irreplaceable role in God's grand narrative. But fulfilling your true destiny starts with discovering your true identity. And therein lies the challenge.

Most of us live our entire lives as strangers to ourselves. We know more about others than we know about ourselves. Our true identities get buried beneath the mistakes we've made, the insecurities we've acquired, and the lies we've believed. We're held captive by others' expectations. We're uncomfortable in our own skin. And we spend far too much emotional, relational, and spiritual energy trying to be who we're not. Why? Because it's easier. And we think it's safer. But trying to be who we're not amounts to forfeiting our spiritual birthrights. It's not just that we're lying to ourselves. Somewhere along the way, we lose ourselves.

I'm not sure where you're at in your journey of self-discovery. Maybe you're on the front end, trying to figure out who you are. Maybe you're on the back end, trying to remember who you were meant to be. Or maybe you're somewhere in between, trying to close the gap between who you are and who you want to be. No matter where you are, I want you to experience the joy of discovering *who you are* and the freedom of discovering *who you're not*. It won't be easy. And there are no shortcuts. But if you are breathing, God hasn't given up on you yet. So don't give up on yourself. Let this promise soak into your spirit, because it will energize your reading: *it's never too late to be who you might have been.*

SECOND PERSONA

Self-discovery is a lot like an archaeological dig. It takes a long time to uncover the hidden treasures that lie buried beneath the surface. You can never be certain of what you will find or where you will find it. And it is a painstaking process. But the failure to dig deep will result in a superficial life. If you live as a stranger to yourself, how can you find intimacy with others? Intimacy is a function of self-discovery. It's hard to truly get to know others if you don't even know yourself. And beyond the relational ramifications, there are occupational implications. If you haven't discovered your unique gifts and passions, how can you find fulfillment in what you do? You might make a living, but you won't make a life. You'll never experience the joy of doing what you love and loving what you do. And, finally, it's the spiritual side effects of superficiality that are the most detrimental. Superficiality is a form of hypocrisy. If you fail to discover the truth, the whole truth, about yourself, aren't you lying to yourself? Your life becomes a half truth.

I live in a city, Washington DC, where image is everything. Meg Greenfield, who spent thirty years covering the city as a journalist with the *Washington Post*, likened it to high school. She referred to high school as a "preeminently nervous" place, and she believed that Washington was even worse. "High school is the time when people first contrive to have an image," observed Greenfield. "It is an attempt to fabricate a whole second persona for public consumption." And it's that second persona that results in a secondhand life. Instead of narrating our own lines in the first person, we live second-person lives by allowing others to narrate our lives for us. And that is hypocrisy at its worst. Our lives become lies. We not only cheat ourselves and others when we fail to discover our God-given identities and God-ordained destinies, but we also cheat God Himself. Greenfield wrote:

Life inside the image…requires continuous care, feeding,
and, above all, protection. That is the worst of it…. It's
like never being able to get undressed….

We are, most of us, much of the time, in disguise.
We present ourselves as we think we are meant to be.
In Washington this is greatly in excess of the ordinary
hypocrisies…that exist everywhere else.[1]

I wish this were true only in Washington, but it's everywhere. In fact, superficiality is the curse of our culture. And the primary reason we live as strangers to ourselves is because we're afraid of what we'll find if we start digging. We don't really want to see ourselves for who we are. But if we can dig deeper than our fallen natures, we'll find the truth that lies buried beneath our sin: the image of God. We'll find our true identities. And our true destinies as well.

In the pages that follow, we'll dig into your past, looking for clues to your future. We'll dust off the lies you've believed and insecurities you've acquired until your true identity is unveiled. And we'll make discoveries, both painful and pleasurable, that will forever change the way you see yourself. In fact, you'll never see yourself the same way, because you'll see yourself through the eyes of your Creator.

DESTINY CLUES

Time may be measured in minutes, but life is measured in moments. And some moments are larger than life. And it's those defining moments that dictate the way we see life. Some of them are as predictable as a wedding day or the birth of a child. Others are as unpredictable as an accident. You never know which moment might become a defining moment, but identifying those moments is the key to identifying who you are.

Psychological research suggests that one's self-concept is defined by a very small number of experiences. Ninety-nine percent of life's experiences vanish like vapor into the subconscious abyss. Only one percent make it into our conscious memories. And less than one percent of that one percent are not just memorable but truly unforgettable. Those are the moments that define us. And managing those memories is a form of stewardship. Every past experience is preparation for some future opportunity. And one way God redeems the past is by helping us see it through His eyes, His providence. So the key to fulfilling your future destiny is hidden in your past memories.

When we look in the mirror, what we see is a reflection of our accumulated experiences. And defining moments are like defining features. In a sense, we are an aggregation of where we've been, what we've done, and who we've known. But there are a few places, a few experiences, and a few people that leave their imprints in ways that become parts of our soulprints.

Exactly what, you may be wondering, is a soulprint? Think of it this way: Your fingerprint uniquely identifies you and differentiates you from everyone else who has ever lived, but your fingerprint is only skin deep. You possess a uniqueness that is soul deep.

I call it your soulprint. It's not just who you are, present tense. It's who you are destined to become, future tense. It's not just who others see when they look at you from the outside in. It's who God has destined you to become from the inside out. Not unlike your genetic code that programs your physical anatomy, your soulprint hardwires your true identity and true destiny. So while you live your life forward, God works backward. The Omniscient One always starts with the end in mind.

The best example of how God uses defining moments to reveal a person's destiny is found in the life of David. He wrote,

> All the days ordained for me
> were written in your book
> before one of them came to be.[2]

As with the psalmist, all your days are ordained by God. And it's your holy responsibility to discover that God-ordained destiny, just like David did. His epitaph speaks for itself:

> When David had served God's purpose in his own
> generation, he fell asleep.[3]

Despite humble beginnings and huge mistakes, David fulfilled his destiny. And that's why David's life is the backdrop for this book. He is the soulprint prototype. The defining moments or scenes in his life double as destiny clues that will help you serve

God's unique purpose in your generation. In the pages that follow, we will dissect David's life in a way that will help you discover your own destiny.

On the most memorable day of his life, David bent down by a brook that didn't just bisect a battlefield. It bisected his life. His life would never be the same after that day, and he knew it. His life was about to end or about to begin.

Giant footsteps got louder as Goliath drew nearer, but it didn't disrupt David's laserlike focus. Like a child trying to find a flat stone for skipping, David was searching for smooth stones from the riverbed. He knew that the shape of the stone would determine the trajectory of the sling. Then David had a moment, a defining moment. As he bent down by the brook, he saw a reflection of himself in the water, and it was like he was seeing himself for the first time. Everybody who had ever known David, including his own father, saw David as nothing more than a shepherd boy. But as David stared at his reflection in the water, his true identity was revealed. David saw the person God had destined him to become: a giant killer. That was his true identity. That was his true destiny.

Like the ripple effect created by David as he reached into the river, there are defining moments that reverberate down the years of our lives. In fact, they forever change the trajectory of our lives. That's what this book is about—identifying the defining moments that reveal our destinies. We'll think of the five defining moments from David's life as those five smooth stones he picked up that day. And while you may have a few more or a few less, those defining moments from David's life will help you see your own reflection more clearly.

IMMAGINE DEL CUORE

To the average eye, it was a mutilated piece of marble. The aborted sculpture had been abandoned half a century earlier by Agostino di Duccio, but a young artist named Michelangelo saw something in that stone others did not. Chiseling the eighteen-foot block of marble would consume nearly four years of his life, but that seemingly worthless stone was destined to become what many consider the greatest statue ever sculpted by human hands. Giorgio Vasari, a sixteenth-century artist and author, called it nothing less than a miracle. Michelangelo resurrected a dead stone and, breathing his artistry into it, brought *David* into existence.

As he chiseled, Michelangelo envisioned what he called the *immagine del cuore,* or image of the heart. He believed the masterpiece was already inside the stone. All he had to do was remove the excess stone so *David* could escape. He didn't see what was. He saw what could be, what already lay within his heart. He didn't see the imperfections in the stone. He saw a masterpiece of unparalleled beauty. And that is precisely how the Artist sees you.

> *We are God's masterpiece. He has created us anew in Christ Jesus, so we can do the good things he planned for us long ago.*[4]

Every work of art originates in the imagination of the artist. And so you originated in the imagination of God. Awesome thought, isn't it? You were conceived by God long before you were conceived by your parents. You took shape in the imagination of the Almighty before you took shape in your mother's womb. You are His "masterpiece," from the Greek word *poiema*. And it's where we get our English word *poem*. But it refers to any work of art.

You are His painting.

You are His novel.

You are His sculpture.

"Christ is more of an artist than the artists," observed Vincent van Gogh. "He works in the living spirit and the living flesh; he makes men instead of statues." God is painting a picture of grace on the canvas of your life. God is writing His-story, history with a hyphen, through your life. God is crafting your character through the circumstances of your life. To see yourself as anything other than God's masterpiece is to devalue and distort your true identity. And it's in discovering your true identity that your true destiny is revealed.

A sense of destiny is your sacred birthright as a child of God. And it's anchored to the truth found in Ephesians 2:10, quoted on the previous page. The word "planned" is drawn from the Eastern custom of sending servants in advance of a king to prepare the road ahead. It was their responsibility to secure safe passage and make sure the king got to his destination. Paul took that ancient imagery and turned it upside down, or maybe I should say, right side up. The King of kings goes before His servants to prepare the road ahead. In other words, He strategically positions us in the right place at the right time. God is setting you up. And that ought to fill you with an unshakable sense of destiny.

DUAL DESTINY

Michelangelo's masterpiece *David* is enshrined at the Galleria dell'Accademia in Florence, Italy. And thousands of tourists wait for hours every day to get a glimpse. But many of them fail to notice the series of unfinished sculptures that line the corridor on the way to David. Like petrified prisoners, their forms are identifiable—a hand here, a torso there, a protruding leg or part of a head. The statues were intended to adorn the tomb of Pope Julius II, but they are *non finiti*. It's almost as if those sculptures are trying to break free and become what they were intended to be, but they are stuck in stone. Michelangelo called them captives.

Have you ever felt like a captive? You can't seem to break free from habitual sins that have held you back and held you down? A dream God conceived in your spirit years ago hasn't taken shape the way you wanted it to? You know who you want to be, what you want to do, and where you want to go, but you can't seem to get there. I have no idea where you're stuck or for how long you've been stuck. But I do know that God wants to finish what He started.

In His first sermon, Jesus stated His mission in no uncertain terms: to set the captives free.[5] We tend to think of that statement in judicial terms. Salvation is our Get Out of Jail Free card. But it's much more than that. Maybe we should think of that statement in artistic terms. Jesus didn't die just to get us off the hook. He also died to resurrect the person we were destined to be before sin distorted the image of God in us.

And He doesn't just set us free spiritually. He also sets us free emotionally and relationally and intellectually. We are held captive by so many things. We're held captive by our imperfections and insecurities. We're held captive by our guilt and anxiety. We're held captive by expectations and lies and mistakes. Jesus died to set us free from all the above. He doesn't just set us free from who we were. He sets us free to become who we were meant to be. Salvation is not the end goal. Salvation is a new beginning. When we give our lives to Christ, God goes to work. He begins using our circumstances, no matter what circumstances those may be, to chisel us into His image.

When it comes to the will of God, we tend to focus on *what* and *where*. But *what you are doing* or *where you are going* are secondary issues. God's primary concern is *who you're becoming*. It has nothing to do with circumstances. It has everything to do with the character of Christ being formed within you until you look and act and feel and talk and dream and love just like Jesus. The end goal is not a revelation of who *you* are. The end goal is a revelation of who God is. After all, you won't find yourself until you find God. The only way to discover *who you are* is to discover *who God is,* because you're made in His image.

You have a dual destiny. One destiny is universal: to be conformed to the image of Christ. To follow Christ is to become like

Him. That is our chief objective in life: to be just like Jesus. But our other destiny is unique to each of us: to be unlike anyone who has ever lived. Those two destinies may seem to be at odds with each other, but they are anything but. To become like Christ is to become unlike anyone else. He sets us free from who we're not, so we can become who we were destined to be.

INCALCULABLY UNIQUE

As you may recall from a high school biology class, you have forty-six chromosomes. Twenty-three are from your father, and twenty-three are from your mother. And it's that unique combination of chromosomes that determines everything from the color of your eyes to the number of hairs on your head. Your identity is part heredity. And so it is with the image of God. The image of God is both your heredity and your destiny.

The mathematical probability that you would get the exact twenty-three chromosomes you got from your mother is .5 to the twenty-third power. That's 1 in 10 million. But the same is true for the twenty-three chromosomes you got from your father. So if you multiply those two together, the probability that you would be you is 1 in 100 trillion. But you also have to factor in that your parents' chromosomal history had the same probability, and their parents, and their parents' parents. My point? You are incalculably unique.

All of us start out as one-of-a-kind originals, but too many of us end up as carbon copies of someone else. Instead of celebrating our uniqueness, and the uniqueness of others, we're too often threatened by it. We forfeit our uniqueness because we want to fit in. Instead of daring to be different, we sacrifice our soulprints on the altar of conformity.

In one of his best-known essays, "Self-Reliance," Ralph Waldo Emerson wrote, "There is a time in every man's education when he arrives at the conviction that...imitation is suicide. He must take himself for better, for worse." I think that is precisely what David did as he prepared to duel Goliath:

> *Then Saul dressed David in his own tunic. He put a coat of armor on him and a bronze helmet on his head. David fastened on his sword over the tunic and tried walking around, because he was not used to them.*[6]

Arming a warrior for battle was a major ritual in David's day. Armor was an extension of the warrior's character. David could have gone into battle dressed like a king. But David said, "I cannot go in these, because I am not used to them."[7] So he took them off.

What if David had gone out to meet Goliath on Goliath's terms—fully armored, fully armed? I think David would have lost because David wasn't a swordsman. In fact, he probably had never touched a sword in his life.[8] For better or for worse, David was a shepherd. The sword would have posed a greater threat to David, via self-inflicted wounds, than it did to Goliath. But David was deadly with a slingshot.

David came to a crossroads. He had a choice to make. And it

was a choice that would determine his destiny. He could go into battle as Saul—wear Saul's armor, wield Saul's sword, hold Saul's shield. Or he could go into battle as himself—a shepherd with a slingshot. David decided not to don Saul's armor or brandish Saul's sword for one very good reason: he wasn't Saul. David decided to be David. And we're faced with the same decision. There comes a point in all of our lives where we need the courage to take off Saul's armor. And it's the rarest form of courage. It's the courage to be yourself.

THE GREATEST REGRET

On a recent vacation that took my family through the Black Hills of South Dakota, our first stop was the Crazy Horse Memorial. In 1948, Korczak Ziółkowski was commissioned by Lakota chief Henry Standing Bear to design a mountain carving that would honor the famous war leader. The great irony, if you know your history, is that Crazy Horse never allowed himself to be photographed. I wonder what he would have thought about his 563-foot-high statue on the granite face of the Black Hills. Ziółkowski invested more than thirty years of his life carving the statue that is intended to be eight feet higher than the Washington Monument and nine times larger than the faces on Mount Rushmore. Following his death in 1982, Ziółkowski's family has carried on the vision their father started. Their projected completion date is 2050.

That vision, carving what will be the largest sculpture in the world, begs this question: why spend a lifetime carving one larger-than-life statue? In the words of Ziółkowski, "When your life is over, the world will ask you only one question: Did you do what you were supposed to do?"

Why do composers write music? Why do athletes compete? Why do politicians run for office? Why do entrepreneurs start businesses? Why do doctors practice medicine? Why do teachers teach?

There are certainly lots of answers to those questions, but the right answer is this: they do it to give expression to something that is deep within their souls. That something is the soulprint. We find fulfillment in doing what we were originally designed and ultimately destined to do. The song or box score or legislation or company or surgery or curriculum is more than the work of our hands. It's an expression of our souls. It's a reflection of our soulprints.

The failure to give expression to our soulprints will result in our greatest regrets. What a person can become, he or she must become, or be miserable. It's the only way to be true to ourselves and, more important, true to God. "The deepest form of despair," warned Søren Kierkegaard, "is to choose to be another than oneself."

At the end of the day, God isn't going to ask, "Why weren't you more like Billy Graham or Mother Teresa?" He won't even ask, "Why weren't you more like David?" God is going to ask, "Why weren't you more like you?"

Holy Confidence

David was the youngest [brother]. The three oldest followed Saul, but David went back and forth from Saul to tend his father's sheep at Bethlehem.

—1 SAMUEL 17:14–15

Around the turn of the twentieth century, a pioneering psychologist named Alfred Adler proposed the counterintuitive theory of compensation. Adler believed that perceived disadvantages often prove to be disguised advantages because they force us to develop attitudes and abilities that would have otherwise gone undiscovered. And it's only as we compensate for those disadvantages that our greatest gifts are revealed. Seventy percent of the art students that Adler studied had optical anomalies. He observed that some of history's greatest composers, Mozart and Beethoven among them, had degenerative traces in their ears. And he cited a multiplicity of other examples, from a wide variety of vocations, of those who leveraged their weaknesses by discovering new strengths. Adler concluded that perceived disadvantages, such as birth defects, physical ailments, and poverty, can be springboards to success. And that success is not achieved *in spite* of those perceived disadvantages. It's achieved *because* of them.

Subsequent studies have added credibility to Adler's theory. In one study of small-business owners, for example, 35 percent of them were self-identified dyslexics.[1] While none of us would wish dyslexia on our children, because of the academic handicap that comes with it, that disadvantage forced this group of entrepreneurs to cultivate different skill sets. Some of them became more proficient at oral communication because reading was so difficult. Others learned to rely on well-developed social skills to compensate for the challenges they faced in the classroom. And all of them cultivated a work ethic that might have remained dormant if reading had come easy for them.

Our greatest advantages may not be what we perceive as our greatest advantages. Our greatest advantages may actually be hidden in our greatest disadvantages, if we learn to leverage them. And one key to discovering your soulprint is identifying those disadvantages via careful, and sometimes painful, self-inventory.

Your destiny is hidden in your history, but it's often hidden where you would least expect to find it. It isn't just revealed in your natural gifts and abilities; it is also revealed in the compensatory skills you had to develop because of the disadvantages you had to overcome.

When I was starting out in ministry, I was frustrated by the fact that I had to preach from a manuscript. I had friends who could preach from an outline or just jot down a few notes on a note card. I couldn't speak extemporaneously. I had to study longer hours and read more books. Then I had to script and rescript every single word. I would often stay up till three o'clock on Sunday mornings, putting the finishing touches on my manuscripts, and that was after working on the message for more than twenty hours during the week. I thought that my inability to speak extemporaneously was a handicap, but what I perceived as a preaching disadvantage proved to be a writing advantage. Those sermon manuscripts, after some adaptations and alterations, became book manuscripts. And without that perceived disadvantage, I don't think I would have cultivated my writing gifts. Writing, for me, is a compensatory skill.

When was the last time you praised God for your perceived disadvantages or thanked God for the challenges in your life? Without them, we'd never discover or develop the compensatory skills that God wants to use to catapult us spiritually, relationally, and occupationally. Our strengths are hidden within our weaknesses. Our advantages are hidden within our disadvantages. And no one is a better example of that than the king who came disguised as a shepherd. His greatest advantage was the direct result of a perceived disadvantage. And without that disadvantage, he would have never fulfilled his destiny.

FLASHBACK

Let me set the scene.

The clock is ticking, and David's mind is racing. Like a flash flood, memories from the past cascade into his consciousness. David is only a teenager, but his short life flashes before his eyes. That is what happens when you're staring death in the face. In this instance, death is a nine-foot giant named Goliath.

David is googling past experiences in hopes of finding something, anything, that will help him in his present predicament. And that's when it happens. Something triggers a memory. It may be the angle of the sun or the sound of a snapping twig or the breeze blowing in from hills, but whatever it is, David has a flashback. A roaring lion pounces into his mind, looking just as ferocious as it did the day he was tending his father's sheep on the outskirts of Bethlehem. A rush of adrenaline pumps through his veins as he recalls putting a smooth stone in his slingshot. David calms his nerves, steadies his hand, and takes aim at the lion's forehead. The stone hits the target, stunning the lion just long enough to allow David to finish him off with his bare hands.

In that moment, in this memory, fear evaporates and confidence condensates. It's more than a realization. It's a revelation. It's more than self-confidence. It's holy confidence. The uncircumcised Philistine that is staring him down is no different from the wild animals David faced and fought while tending sheep. David connects the dots between his past experiences and his present circumstances, and it inflates his soul with a sense of destiny.

> *Your servant has been keeping his father's sheep. When a lion or a bear came and carried off a sheep from the flock, I went after it, struck it and rescued the sheep from its mouth. When it turned on me, I seized it by its hair, struck it and killed it. Your servant has killed both the lion and the bear; this uncircumcised Philistine will be like one of them, because he has defied the armies of the living God. The LORD who delivered me from the paw of the lion and the paw of the bear will deliver me from the hand of this Philistine.*[2]

Every past experience is preparation for some future opportunity. God doesn't just redeem our souls. He also redeems our experiences. And not just the good ones. He redeems the bad ones too—especially the bad ones. How? By cultivating character, developing gifts, and teaching lessons that cannot be learned any other way. The most important lessons in life are rarely learned in a school classroom via secondhand knowledge. Relying on secondhand knowledge results in a vicarious life. You become an extra in your own story instead of taking the lead role. The expectations of others become your script. And you live off their experiences instead of creating your own.

The most important lessons are learned in the classroom of life via firsthand experience. The tests are tough, but no curriculum is more effective. And the way you pass the test is by cultivating the character, developing the gift, or learning the lesson God is trying to teach you through that experience. One thing that has helped me endure the challenges I've faced is seeing each of them as learning opportunities. If you learn the lesson God is trying to teach you, no matter how things turn out, you have not failed. In fact, you cannot fail.

Each wild animal that attacked David's flock was a pop quiz. They tested his character and his skill. David could have sacrificed his sheep for the sake of personal safety, but he passed the test by risking his life for his flock. Why is that so significant? Because God was preparing David to shepherd His flock, the nation of Israel. He was also cultivating a compensatory skill that would change David's destiny and Israel's history.

On paper, David was at an obvious disadvantage. He wasn't even in the army! If anyone was going to face Goliath, it would be a trained soldier, right? His brothers seemed more qualified than David. David didn't even know how to wield a sword or throw a spear. All he'd been doing was tending sheep. But that perceived disadvantage gave him the advantage he needed to defeat Goliath. Israelite soldiers were trained the same way the Philistines were. And no one was going to defeat Goliath in hand-to-hand combat. No one, especially not David, could match Goliath's strength or his skill. You cannot fight a giant on the giant's terms. You have to change the rules of engagement. The best way to fight a giant is with a slingshot at twenty paces. And that is a skill shepherds cultivate out of necessity. So while it seems as if David was totally unprepared, he was actually perfectly prepared. And while it seems as if he was in the wrong place at the wrong time, David was perfectly positioned.

SIDELINES

When I was in high school, I played basketball for a coach who, like every coach, had his idiosyncrasies. During my junior year, I was coming off the bench as a sixth man, so I was always fighting for playing time, and I quickly learned that our coach would pull players out of the game when they made mistakes. Here's how he would do it: he would just grab whoever was next to him on the bench, send him to the scorer's table, and get him into the game as quickly as possible. If you were at the end of the bench, you were out of sight, out of mind. So, during huddles, when our team would get off the bench, I always tried to get the spot next to our coach when we sat back down. It was like athletic musical chairs. I got a lot of playing time that year by virtue of my strategic positioning.

Like any athlete, I hated sitting on the sidelines. I wanted to get into the game. I wanted to contribute to our team. I wanted to help us win. But you can't do that if you aren't on the court. For anyone with a competitive streak, there is nothing worse than getting stuck on the bench. And I wonder if that is how David felt as he watched his brothers go off to war. He wanted to go with them. He wanted to be on the front lines, but he got stuck on the sidelines. He wanted to be on the battlefield, but he got stuck in the shepherd's field. But if we learn anything from this scene in David's life, it's this: The battle with Goliath wasn't won in the Valley of Elah. It was won on the hillsides on the outskirts of Bethlehem.

David must have felt like he had been put out to pasture. What a letdown when he was passed over during the draft. But what David didn't realize at the time was that God was getting him ready to go into the game. And that is how God is working in your life. He is preparing you for your date with destiny. I promise you that. But I also promise that He's doing it in ways that are virtually undetectable. And it's not until you find yourself facing the biggest challenge of your life that God reveals how and when and where He prepared you. That's when you recognize that the battle isn't won on the battlefield. It's won or lost long before that.

There is a time to be on the front lines, but there is also a time to be on the sidelines. There is a time to be in the limelight, but there is also a time to be in the shadows. Moses needed to tend sheep for forty years before he could lead the flock of Israel. The disciples needed to fish for fish before they could fish for men. And even Jesus needed to craft masterpieces in wood before He made masterpieces out of us. Every divine appointment is preceded by a season of preparation. And if we submit to the preparation, God will fulfill His promise. If we don't, He won't. Why? Because God never sets us up to fail.

I went to a hundred conferences before I ever spoke at one. I read thousands of books before I ever wrote one. And I wouldn't trade those seasons on the sidelines. I wouldn't want to go back to the days when I was a one-man staff preaching sermons, leading worship, copying bulletins, counseling couples, answering phones, editing videos, and organizing outreaches. But I wouldn't trade that season either. It's the time we spend on the sidelines that prepares us for the front lines. Even first-round draft picks with amazing athletic skills need to spend some time on the sidelines learning the nuances of the game at the NFL level. It's the players who redeem the time on the sidelines who set themselves up for success when they eventually get on the field.

One key to fulfilling your destiny is recognizing what season you are in. If you don't, you'll experience high levels of frustration and disappointment. For example, there are seasons when learning to lead isn't as important as learning to follow. There are seasons when handling failure is of greater value than handling success. I tell every church planter I meet that the first five years don't count, because God has to grow the leader before He can grow whatever it is that person is leading. Don't worry about church growth. If you're growing personally, church growth will take care of itself.

One of the biggest mistakes we make is focusing all our energy on the next season of life instead of enjoying the season we're in. And I see an obvious manifestation of that in the congregation I pastor. Our church is 70 percent single twenty-somethings. Many of them want to be playing the dating game, but they're playing the waiting game instead. They want to be on the dating front lines, but they are stuck on the sidelines. Here's my perennial advice: don't focus on finding the right person; focus on becoming the right person. It's not about finding Ms. Right. It's about becoming Mr. Right. In God's grand scheme, it's never about orchestrating the right circumstances. It's always about becoming the right person. And sometimes the worst of circumstances brings out the best in us! So what we perceive as the wrong circumstance can actually produce something right—or righteous—in us.

DIVINE DELAYS

I have two primary callings: pastoring and writing. But the routes by which I arrived at each destiny were very different. The path to pastoring was a direct path, while the path to writing was full of dead ends. Half a dozen manuscripts miscarried before I finally published my first book. I felt called to write when I was in seminary, but it took thirteen years to accomplish that calling. I can't even put into words the frustration I felt, and it got worse every year. I hated celebrating my birthday because it was an annual reminder that one more year had passed without fulfilling my destiny. During one season of acute frustration, I asked God to take away the desire and the dream. But He didn't do it. Have you ever been there? Your dream seems like a mirage that remains the same distance away no matter how fast or how far you pursue it. You know you have a destiny to fulfill, but the elapsed time causes you to second-guess yourself.

I was about ready to give up on the writing dream when I decided to give it one last shot. I leveraged my birthday as a self-imposed deadline. I did a forty-day fast to focus my energies. And I finally self-published my first book right before my thirty-fifth birthday. Getting my first book into print was more of a relief than anything else. I didn't really rejoice. It simply alleviated the frustration I had felt for so many years. A few years have passed since that book was published, and my perception of that delayed dream is now very different. I'm so grateful it took so long! Here's why: if I had written my first book at twenty-five instead of thirty-five, it would have been all theory and no substance. I hadn't lived enough life. I would have been writing out of secondhand knowledge instead of firsthand experience. And my books would have lacked the credibility that comes with experience.

We hate to wait. We want our dreams to become reality yesterday. But I've come to appreciate what I now call divine delays.

God wants you to get where God wants you to go more than you want to get where God wants you to go. So take a deep breath, enjoy the journey, and know that God will get you there when you're ready to get there. Your current frustration will be cause for future celebration if you hang in there long enough. Don't give up! God is building emotional endurance. And the key to emotional endurance is experiencing high levels of disappointment that break us down so God can build us back up with a holy confidence. Anytime I feel stretched emotionally, I remind myself that God is expanding my emotional capacity to be used by Him in greater ways.

In recent months I've experienced a couple of major disappointments. The first one involved a piece of property for our church that I thought was the Promised Land. I'd prayed on it, around it, and over it for months. I really thought it would belong to National Community Church. We actually had a contract, with two out of three necessary signatures. All it required was a signature from the third partner, but we never got the third signature. At the eleventh hour, we lost the property to a real-estate developer. I had invested so much emotional and spiritual energy in the project that I felt catatonic afterward. It seemed like that dream was dead, but sometimes what we perceive as a death is really a divine delay.

We so quickly forget the central fact of our faith: without a crucifixion there is no resurrection. Those days between death and resurrection are long and dark, but that's often when a miracle is about to happen. You never know how or when or where a dream will be resurrected, but if it's God ordained, then God Himself will bring it back to life somehow, somewhere, sometime.

The other disappointment involves a life goal. My daughter, Summer, and I recently flew out to San Francisco to do the Alcatraz Sharkfest Swim. We had trained for months, flew cross-country to get there, and invested quite a bit of money on everything from wetsuits to accommodations. On the morning of the race, we got registered, marched from the Aquatic Park to Pier 33, and hopped on the ferry to Alcatraz Island. The adrenaline was pumping as we prepared to swim 1.5 miles through freezing-cold, shark-infested waters. I was in the zone. This goal ranked as one of the most challenging and dangerous I'd ever attempted. And I knew it would be an amazing shared experience for Summer and me. I wanted to show her that she was capable, even at a young age, of far more than she imagined.

Then, just as we were getting ready to jump off the boat and into the water, the captain's voice came over the intercom and in-formed us that the race had been canceled because of fog. I hon-estly thought it was a joke, a bad joke. After all, San Francisco is always foggy! I didn't even know that cancellation was a possibil-ity. When I realized it wasn't a joke, I was devastated. I realize that a cancelled race doesn't rank high on the spiritual-significance scale. But it was one of the biggest emotional letdowns I've ever experienced.

I'm still getting over the residual disappointment, but I'm not giving up on that goal. I can't control what happened, but I can control my reaction to it. That goal isn't dead. It's just delayed.

And instead of causing me to give in to defeatism, the delay steels my determination. Accomplishing that goal will taste even sweeter when it's finally achieved.

Like David watching his brothers go off to war, maybe you feel overlooked and underappreciated. It seems like everyone else is getting the promotion, getting the scholarship, or getting the girl (or the guy). Your day will come. In the meantime, don't short-circuit His plans and purposes by taking shortcuts. God is setting you up. He is making divine appointments. But the bigger the opportunity, the longer it takes. The reason we get frustrated is because we think big without thinking long. That is a recipe for disappointment. Reevaluate your timeline. And be encouraged when it takes longer than you expected. That simply means that God wants to do something immeasurably more than all you can ask or imagine.

COMPENSATORY SKILLS

Michelangelo's *David* is a towering presence, fourteen feet tall from head to toe. The real David? You'd probably be looking down. David wasn't just the youngest of nine brothers. The language in the Bible story seems to suggest that David may also have been the smallest in stature. The Hebrew word for "youngest" isn't just chronological. It's also physical. David was the runt of the litter in every sense of the phrase. David looked like anything *but* a warrior. That's why Saul questioned his credentials and Goliath mocked his opponent. But David possessed a skill as a shepherd that the soldiers did not. While they were trained in their traditional boot camp, David was trained in ancient guerrilla warfare. His training ground was the hillsides where his flock grazed. His target practice was the wild animals that attacked his flock. And his compensatory skill was using a slingshot. David had no idea that God would use a shepherding skill to catapult him into the national limelight. And we've heard the story so many times that we take it for granted, but David was the unlikeliest of heroes with the unlikeliest of skills. If David isn't an expert marksman with a slingshot, there is no way he defeats Goliath; he most definitely doesn't become king; and he therefore never produces a royal lineage that includes the Messiah.

One of the story lines in this scene is the way God used a seemingly random skill to strategically position David. And the slingshot skill isn't the only example. I bet David complained about taking music lessons as a kid. I know I did. I actually gave up the bass because it was just too big to carry back and forth to school. Try a harp! But those music lessons paid off for David. It was his skill with the harp that opened the palace doors in the first place.[3] When David played the harp, it soothed Saul's spirit. That's how David met Jonathan. That's how he learned the customs of the court. Without his musical skills, David wouldn't have even gotten a foot in the door!

You never know what skill God will use for His purposes, so don't underestimate the strangest of skills. God can use anything and everything for His purposes if we simply allow ourselves to be used by Him. God used Noah's boat-building skills, Joseph's ability to interpret dreams, Esther's face and figure, and the Magi's astrological knowledge. No skill is unredeemable or unusable in God's grand scheme.

It was his skill with a slingshot that netted David his first fifteen minutes of fame. But it was another compensatory skill, maybe his greatest skill, that translated into three thousand years of cumulative influence. David was more than a musical performer. He was a songwriter. And those songs, called psalms, still rank as the most popular portion of the most popular book of all time. But here's what you need to see: the greatest of psalms came out of the worst circumstances. Or to put it another way, the most comforting psalms were written in the most uncomfortable situations. David is walking through the valley of the shadow of death. David is agonizing over his adulterous affair with Bathsheba. David is a fugitive hiding out in the caves of Adullam. David didn't want to be in any of those situations, but those circumstances produced the profound lyrics we find in Psalm 23, Psalm 51, and Psalm 142.

You may not want to be where you are. Maybe you're wrestling with depression or reeling from a mistake that seems unforgivable, or you're just sick and tired of being sick and tired. Dare I suggest that God is cultivating character? How do I know that? Because you are His masterpiece! He is chipping and chiseling. And like a half-finished piece of art, it may not look beautiful yet. But God always finishes what He starts, as long as we don't quit on Him. So you may not like your present circumstances, but they may be the key to your character development. And character development is the key to your future.

I love movies with lots of action and adventure. Give me a few good stunts, some special effects, and a bucket of popcorn with extra butter and I'm a happy camper. But I have to admit, the best movies aren't the movies with the most action. They are the movies with the best characters. And the key is character development. Don't you love movies where the main character has to overcome an obstacle or face a fear or fight an injustice? We love those characters who have to overcome extreme adversity. We just don't want to be them. We want to watch them on a screen. But here's what we need to recognize: it's not the resolution of circumstances, but the evolution of character, that God is after. And the worst circumstances often produce the best character and the best story line. That is certainly true of David. And it's true of you.

CONNECT THE DOTS

Looking back on life is like a game of connect the dots, where the dots are defining moments. Some of them are big dots that stamp our soulprints in indelible ways. Some of them are little dots that shape our subconscious outlook on life. And together, the big dots and little dots reveal the contours of our soulprints.

"There is always one moment in childhood," says Graham Greene, "when the door opens and lets the future in." David's close encounters with lions and bears doubled as defining moments that shaped his outlook on life. How do we know that? Because they were near-death experiences, and nothing stamps the soulprint like a near-death experience. It yields the most valuable lesson.

Here's the lesson David learned: "The LORD who delivered me from the paw of the lion and the paw of the bear will deliver me from the hand of this Philistine."[4] It's a verse of Scripture to us, but it was a defining moment for David. And that defining moment conceived in him a holy confidence. David walked onto the battlefield with an unshakable sense of destiny. It was a big dot.

When I was a sophomore in high school, I took a speech class. I'm not sure why, but when it was time to deliver my first speech, I decided to preach what would amount to my first sermon. I don't think it was a defining moment for anyone in the audience. Let's just say that no one got saved that day! The speech wasn't well organized or well delivered. But that speech was a defining moment for me. In the words of Graham Greene, a door opened and let the future in.

Without my knowledge, my mom gave a copy of that speech to my grandma, who in turn gave a copy to her Bible-study leader. Her Bible-study leader said to my grandma, "Has Mark ever thought about ministry?" That question got relayed to my mom, who relayed the question to me. And the answer to that question? *No.* It had never even crossed my mind…at least not until that moment! And in that moment, a sophomore speech dotted my soulprint.

I'm not sure exactly where I first stumbled across this random claim, but I once read that our outlook on life is determined by a dozen defining moments. Now, I'm not sure that can be quantified or codified. And it may be six or eleven or seventeen defining moments. But I think it's generally true that we are largely shaped by a small handful of experiences. And those shaping experiences are the big and small dots, if you will. Collectively, they form our internal operating system. They are the source code that determines the way we look at life. And if you're going to discover your soulprint, you need to mine your memory for those defining moments.

When connecting the dots, it helps to think about different stages, places, and people. What are your earliest memories? Who were the major influencers in your life? What major events, both good and bad, mark your elementary, junior high, high school, and college years? As you reflect on those memories, what lessons did you learn consciously or subconsciously? What character traits or compensatory skills was God cultivating? What did those experiences reveal to you or about you?

What will surprise you, as you do a little personal archaeology, is the way seemingly insignificant events have shaped your subconscious operating system. What seems insignificant to others can change the entire trajectory of your life. Fleeting thoughts become unforgettable memories. Passing comments have prophetic impact. And seemingly superficial events can result in profound paradigm shifts.

As a kid, I was a huge Vikings fan. I watched the games and collected the cards. I even had a Vikings bathrobe that has been preserved and passed down to the next generation of Battersons. One of my earliest memories is going to my first professional football game at the old Metropolitan Stadium in Bloomington, Minnesota. The Vikings were playing the San Francisco 49ers, and fans were flooding out of the stadium at the end of the third quarter. It seemed like the game was already lost, but we stayed in our seats. Then we got out of our seats as the Vikings scored three touchdowns and pulled off the most amazing fourth-quarter comeback I'd ever witnessed.

That's the day I became a die-hard fan. That's also the day I became an irrepressible optimist. It doesn't matter if my team is behind by two touchdowns with two minutes left. Don't you dare touch the TV! We're not turning it off and we're not changing the channel, because I'm imagining comeback scenarios in my mind. All we have to do is force a turnover, score a touchdown, recover an onside kick, throw a Hail Mary pass, and attempt a two-point conversion. In my mind, it's not over till it's over. In fact, it's never over!

Did I mention that I'm an irrepressible optimist? And I honestly think it traces back to that incredible fourth-quarter comeback I witnessed when I was at an impressionable age. It was a defining moment for me, and that irrepressible optimism translates into every part of my life. I can't give up.

CONTROL ISSUES

Another of the big dots in my life is a near-death experience that happened nearly a decade ago. I had been suffering from abdominal pains for a week, but the doctors couldn't figure out what was wrong. I finally landed in the emergency room at Washington Hospital Center, doubled over in pain. An MRI revealed ruptured intestines. The doctor pulled the curtain at 2:00 a.m., and the look on his face said it all. He told me that I needed to go into surgery immediately. I knew it was a matter of life or death, and part of me was in so much pain that I wanted to die. I would spend the next two days on a respirator fighting for my life.

It was during my recovery from surgery that I picked up a biography of Oswald Chambers. His classic devotional, *My Utmost for His Highest,* is my all-time favorite. But it wasn't until I read his biography, *Abandoned to God,* that I fully appreciated why his writing has such dimensionality. I think it's because he experienced so much suffering and so many setbacks. One reason I identify with Chambers is because he, too, suffered a rupture. In his case, it was a burst appendix. And he actually died from complications. Despite the difficulties and disappointments he endured, Chambers coined one of my favorite mantras: "Let God engineer."[5] Those three words captured his trust in the overarching sovereignty of God. And it's that kind of trust that gives us a holy confidence.

Most of our emotional problems are symptoms of one deep-rooted spiritual problem: lack of trust in the sovereign God. It's our lack of trust in Him that results in high levels of past-tense guilt, present-tense stress, and future-tense anxiety. And if we allow it to, that three-headed monster will deplete every ounce of holy confidence we possess until we lose our sense of destiny.

Many of us find our confidence in the things we can control, but it's a false sense of confidence. Holy confidence isn't circumstantial. It's providential. Too often we allow our circumstances to get between God and us. Holy confidence puts God between us and our circumstances. And when we do that, the Almighty One dwarfs the giants in our lives.

Let's face it: we are control freaks. We want to control our circumstances. We want to control others. And, ultimately, we want to control God Himself. We do this in the name of sanctification, but it's pseudosanctification. It's nothing more, or maybe I should say nothing less, than a futile attempt at self-help. Lack of trust is more than refusing God's help. It's a prideful attempt to help God by doing His job for Him. We play God by trying to control everyone, everything. But God hasn't called us to be God. He's called us to be ourselves. And our control issues are really trust issues. The less we trust God, the more we have to control.

The loss of control feels like a loss of life. And that's how I felt as I lay in my hospital bed after the anesthesia wore off. When you're on a respirator, you realize how little control you actually have. You come face to face with your mortality. But if you survive the scare, it can actually bring you to life in new ways. All of a sudden, I didn't have to pretend that I had everything under control. In fact, I couldn't pretend. Not when I had an IV feeding my veins and oxygen tubes plugging my nose. So while I survived the surgery, my self-confidence did not. And I'm eternally grateful for that.

Nothing is more spiritually, emotionally, or relationally exhausting than pretending you hold the planets in orbit. And the flipside is true as well. The greatest freedom in the world is relinquishing control and submitting your life to the Sovereign One.

And when you do, self-confidence is crucified. But self-confidence must die if holy confidence is to be resurrected. The two cannot coexist.

UNCONQUERABLENESS

Along with coining "Let God engineer," Oswald Chambers also coined one of my all-time favorite words: *unconquerableness.* Chambers took the phrase "more than conquerors"[6] and added a twist. In his words from *My Utmost for His Highest,* "No power on earth or in hell can conquer the Spirit of God in a human spirit, it is an inner unconquerableness."

David had an *unconquerableness* about him. He wouldn't step back or step down. He knew that his duel with Goliath was his date with destiny. He saw the way God had engineered his experiences and orchestrated this opportunity. And God is doing the same in your life. It starts with little opportunities and small victories. God uses them to build confidence. And it's not a self-confidence in your abilities. It's a holy confidence in God's abilities.

In a sense, our faith is really a by-product of God's faithfulness. God proves Himself faithful, and it builds our faith as we connect the dots. We realize that the God who delivered us from the paw of the lion and the paw of the bear will also deliver us from the giants in our lives. And no matter how big the giant, we have an inner unconquerableness. But it always starts with small wins.

Not long ago, Summer ran her first 5K with one of our youth leaders. She started out as a reluctant runner. She wasn't running because she loved running. She was running because she loved her youth leader. At times it was a workout just getting her to work out. But something snapped when she crossed the finish line on race day. She felt the rush of adrenaline that occurs when you go after a goal and accomplish it. The next day, the reluctant runner was talking about doing a half marathon. Of course, the fact that it was the Princess Half Marathon at Disney might have had a little something to do with that. But it's small wins that give us the confidence to go after bigger goals.

And I think that was the case with David. Each wild animal that David defeated gave him a little more holy confidence. By the time he reached the Valley of Elah, he had accumulated enough holy confidence to go after a giant. It takes time. And in your case as in his, you'll lose a few battles along the way. But as you look back on your history, I hope you are able to connect the dots. I hope reviewing your history gives you a sense of destiny. And I hope you are filled with an inner unconquerableness, because He who began a good work in you will carry it on to completion.[7]

God is ordering your footsteps just like He did for David, and you ought to expect some divine delays. But even the disappointments we experience, like David's brothers going off to war while he was stuck shearing sheep, are divine appointments in disguise. And they ought to come with a footnote in fine print: *To be redeemed.*

So let me end with a footnote. Remember the contract our

church lost because we couldn't get the third signature? I was so disappointed we didn't get it then, but I'm so glad we didn't now. I honestly thought that disappointment would be unresolved when this book was published, but right before the final manuscript was due, God came through. We got a contract on another piece of property. It is right across the street from the other property. It is twice as much land. And the cost per square foot was nearly half.

The longer I live, the more I thank God for the disappointments in my life. Those disappointments often prove to be divine appointments. They may come disguised as divine delays or perceived disadvantages. But if you give God a chance, He will redeem your disappointments. Of that you can be sure. And it's that assurance that breeds an inner unconquerableness.

Let God engineer.

Lifesymbols

David took the head of the Philistine and brought it to Jerusalem, but he put his armor in his tent.

—1 SAMUEL 17:54, ESV

Our family recently moved to a new house, and I think we set a U-Haul record for the least mileage on a moving van. It cost $1.59 per mile, so our half-a-block move equated to $0.47 in mileage charges. Of course, that didn't make the move any easier, because we still had to pack and unpack everything we had accumulated during the fourteen years we lived in our first house. During the process of unpacking, I came across an old shoe box that I had not seen in many years. I stopped my frenzied foray and took a leisurely stroll down memory lane. The next hour felt like a lifetime because that shoe box contained a lifetime of memories.

The contents were both worthless and priceless: a Kung Phooey lunchbox that doubled as a sacrosanct container for my vintage football cards; a gold medal from the Awana Olympics; a fourth-grade art project that somehow made the keepsake cut; the flat shoe I wore while recovering from a broken ankle in high school; and an occupational assessment I took in grad school. For the record, I scored well below average in my aptitude for writing. I hope you find as much humor in that as I did.

As I rummaged through old journals and photo albums, I realized that part of me was still in that shoe box. And it reminded me of a book, *Tuesdays with Morrie,* that I had read years before. In it, the author, Mitch Albom, interviews his old college professor, Morrie Schwartz, who shares reflections on life as he fights Lou Gehrig's disease to the death. The book is full of profundities, but the most memorable for me is an exchange about aging. Morrie says to Mitch, "I *embrace* aging. It's very simple. As you grow, you learn more. If you stayed at twenty-two, you'd always be as ignorant as you were at twenty-two." (No offense, twenty-two-year-olds. He said it, not me.) Then Morrie shares a perspective on life that ought to be internalized sooner rather than later or younger rather than older. "The truth is, part of me is every age. I'm a three-year-old, I'm a five-year-old, I'm a thirty-seven-year-old, I'm a fifty-year-old. I've been through all of them, and I know what it's like. I delight in being a child when it's appropriate to be a child. I delight in being a wise old man when it's appropriate to be a wise old man. Think of all I can be! I am every age, up to my own."[1]

As I sorted though my shoe box of memories, I thought of that statement, "I am every age, up to my own." The spiritual mementos inside my shoe box don't just reveal who I was. They reveal who I am, because I am every age up to my own. The oxygen mask from my stint in the ICU is not just a distant memory. It's part of my daily consciousness. I thought I was taking my last breath when a nurse signaled a code blue and placed that oxygen mask over my mouth and nose. And while it happened a long time ago, I'm pretty sure that my intense present-tense love for life traces back to that past-tense, near-death moment. I no longer need that mask physically, but I still need it spiritually.

In a sense, I am that shoe box and that shoe box is me. I am more than my name, more than my occupation, more than my degrees, more than my dreams, more than my family. I am who I was. It's my footprints, where I've been and what I've done, that reveal my soulprint. It's my unique combination of memories that makes me who I am spiritually, emotionally, relationally, and motivationally. It's also that unique combination of memories that enables me to worship God in a way that no one else can. Why? Because when we sing the classic hymn "Great Is Thy Faithfulness," it's more than generic praise for a static character trait. God's faithfulness is as unique as every moment of your life. Every memory is a testament to His dynamic faithfulness that is simultaneously the same and different for anyone and everyone else. So when our congregation sings that hymn, it's not one song. It's hundreds and hundreds of unique songs that harmonize the faithfulness of God.

By nature, I'm a future-tense person. Before we launch one of our church's multisite locations, I'm already thinking about the next one and the one after that. Before one book is released, I start writing the next one. I'm always thinking about what's next. And I thank God for the right-brain imagination that enables me to do this. But without the ability to remember yesterday, the ability to imagine tomorrow would become meaningless. Without memory, we'd have to relearn everything every day. Without memory, we'd forget who we are and where we've been. Without memory, we'd lose faith because we'd forget the faithfulness of God.

THE ART OF ALTAR MAKING

Our defining moments double as altars to God. The stones, like those David used as artillery, turn into stone altars. And while there isn't any biblical proof to this end, I'm guessing David kept the bloodstained stone that was buried in Goliath's forehead. Like David, we need holy keepsakes to remind us of where we've been and where we're headed.

I wonder if Abraham ever journeyed back to Mount Moriah, where God provided a sacrificial ram in the thicket to take the place of his son. Maybe he even kept one of its horns. Did Jacob ever camp out at Bethel again? Do you think Peter ever rowed out to the spot on the Sea of Galilee where he once walked on water? I bet Zacchaeus let his grandkids climb the sycamore tree where he got his first glimpse of Jesus. How many times did Paul travel the road to Damascus and stop at the mile marker where he got knocked off his high horse? And if you were Lazarus, wouldn't you have made an annual trek to the tomb where you were buried for four days? Maybe even put some fresh-cut flowers by your tomb?

I'm afraid that the art of altar making is a lost spiritual discipline. And our loss of long-term memory causes a plethora of acute spiritual problems. The primary reason we lose faith is because we forget the "faith-fullness" of God. Maybe that's why the word *remember* is repeated almost 250 times in Scripture. We have a tendency to remember what we should forget and forget what we should remember. And that's why God is always telling us to build altars or establish memorials. So Jacob builds a dream altar at Bethel. The Israelites take stones from the Jordan River and set them up as a miracle altar in Gilgal. And Samuel builds a victory altar at Mizpah after defeating the Philistines. There may be more memorials in Israel, per square mile, than in Washington, DC. So why do we build them? Why are they such prominent parts of a cityscape or lifescape? Because without those physical reminders, we quickly forget the spiritual lessons we've learned along the way. I call those physical reminders "lifesymbols." And they come in every size and shape imaginable, including oxygen masks.

I'm not the most artistic person on the planet, and you certainly don't want me decorating your home, but a few years ago I had a revelation. I'm not sure where the question came from, but the answer led to an artistic renaissance: *Why am I surrounding myself with meaningless things?* I realized that the art on my walls held no personal meaning to me whatsoever, and I decided to change that. I decided to surround myself with things that remind me of who I am and whose I am. I decided to surround myself with reminders of where I've been and where I'm going. I don't want art on my shelves; I want altars to the faithfulness of God. So in the years since that revelation, I've started accumulating artistic altars that jog my spiritual memory.

My shelves in my office, too, are now full of lifesymbols. I have the liquor bottle we found in the crackhouse that we turned into a coffeehouse. I have an old bathroom sign from the Union Station movie theaters where we met as a church for thirteen years.

I have the *New York Times* article that put our podcast on the map. And I have one of my most treasured possessions, a well-used Bible that belonged to my grandfather. My office isn't an office. It's an altar to the faithfulness of God where I happen to have meetings, check e-mail, and occasionally get work done.

My most significant lifesymbol is a framed photograph of the cow pasture in Alexandria, Minnesota, where I felt called to ministry when I was nineteen years old. A prayer walk through that cow pasture changed the trajectory of my life. It was my burning-bush moment. So a few years ago I took a pilgrimage back there, along with a photographer I hired to snap some stills. Like every other pastor, I have difficult days when I need to be reminded of why I do what I do. Those are the moments when I simply swivel my chair and look back, literally and figuratively, at that picture of that cow pasture. It's like smelling salts to my sense of destiny.

I wonder if that is how David felt every time he saw Goliath's coat of armor hanging in his tent.

125 POUNDS, 15 OUNCES

Let me set the scene.

David knew he hit the bull's-eye, but did he hit it hard enough? He waited for a subtle shift in Goliath's center of balance. That's when intense fear turned into triumphant relief as the nine-foot giant teetered, then came crashing forward like a felled tree. There is an old adage: "The bigger they are, the harder they fall." And it's true. But so is this one: The taller they are, the longer it takes! It takes a long time for giants to hit the ground, but when they do, the cloud of dust is spectacular.

We live in a culture where athletes turn end-zone celebrations into art forms, and I can't help but wonder if David did a little giant-jig as the dust settled. It seems likely given the pregame smack talk between the two. After all, it's tough to contain spontaneous combustions of celebration when improbable victories are won, and David has a long track record of dancing in highly charged emotional moments. While I'm not sure exactly how David celebrated the victory, one thing is certain: David knew who defeated Goliath, and it wasn't him! The victory belonged to the Lord of hosts.

When the giant hit the ground, David didn't waste a moment. He sprinted to the fallen Philistine, unsheathed the giant's sword, and decapitated him with his own weapon. Then David did something curious. He didn't just leave Goliath for a battlefield burial. He began undressing his armor, which was far more complicated than simply untying a shoe or unbuckling a belt. It took all his strength just to turn Goliath over! But piece by piece, David removed the armor that was defenseless against a perfectly aimed stone. The great irony is that removing his armor was more difficult than defeating Goliath. David barely broke a sweat slinging the stone, but removing the giant's armor left him breathless.

It's not insignificant that Scripture records the actual weight of Goliath's armor: 125 pounds, 15 ounces. David probably didn't weigh much more than that! Carrying Goliath's armor was like bench-pressing his own body weight. It wasn't as simple as picking it up and plopping it down in his tent. And it certainly didn't fit on the mantel. It probably took two men just to move it. David's shoe box was much heavier than mine! But David went to the trouble of putting that set of armor in his tent. Every time he packed up his tent and pitched it someplace else, the armor went with him. How come? Because that armor doubled as a daily reminder of a defining moment. It was a 125-pound, 15-ounce lifesymbol. And every time the sunlight reflected off the bronze scales and caught the corner of David's eye, it renewed David's holy confidence in the God who fells giants. And that's the purpose of lifesymbols. They are physical objects that remind of us spiritual milestones. They are reminders from the past that give meaning to the present and holy confidence for the future.

FIRST FUNERAL

I discovered the power and importance of lifesymbols the day I did my first funeral. I was twenty-two years old. The funeral was for my sister-in-law's grandmother. And the circumstances were somewhat strange. Hilma was cremated before Thanksgiving, but the family waited until Christmas to bury the ashes. During the interim, Hilma's son was in charge of the cremation box. But where do you store a cremation box? One day, after his broken-down car had been hooked up to a tow truck, he remembered that the box was in the trunk. That's when he told the driver to wait a moment because he had to get his mother out of the trunk. He probably should have stated it differently! Then he decided to put the box by the Christmas tree, but the dog wouldn't stop sniffing it. I'm sure poor little Pooky was utterly confused: *I know I smell her, but how could she possibly be in such a small box!*

The day of the funeral finally arrived, and I delivered a short graveside message. Because the funeral was so many weeks after Hilma's passing, I felt as if the family wasn't feeling the acute grief that typically accompanies a burial. In fact, the family wasn't expressing much emotion at all until I pulled out a pair of hand-knitted slippers from the inside pocket of my overcoat. When I did, it was like an emotional dam burst, and a flood of tears followed. Christmas is characterized by surprises that come wrapped in paper, but for Hilma's family, one gift was a given. Every member of the family knew that every Christmas they'd get a pair of hand-knitted slippers. Their closets were full of them! Those hand-knitted slippers were the kind of gift you may not like but you love, you may not use but you appreciate, you may not want but you need for nonutilitarian reasons. It would have been much easier for Hilma to give everyone a gift card. And that gift card would have been far more practical. But it also would have been much less meaningful. When Hilma gave those hand-knitted slippers to each member of the family, she was giving herself. The reason the family lost it when they saw those slippers is that those slippers symbolized how much Hilma loved her family. Those slippers were inanimate objects, but they were animated with memories and emotions that are impossible to put into words. Those slippers symbolized who Hilma was and how much she meant to her family. And that's what turns ordinary objects into lifesymbols.

Not long after that funeral, the concept of lifesymbols was crystallized in my spirit when I heard author and speaker Denis Waitley share about an experience that marked his life forever. Denis was trying to catch a flight for a speaking engagement, but he was running late, so he was literally running through the airport terminal. He got to the gate the split second the gate agent closed the door. Denis explained his predicament, but the agent didn't budge despite his begging. That's when his frustration turned into fuming. He stormed out of the boarding area and back to the ticket counter to register a complaint and reschedule his flight. The anger intensified as he waited for more than twenty minutes in a line that barely moved. Just before he got to the ticket counter, an announcement over the intercom changed his life, because he realized that missing that flight had saved his life. The flight he missed, flight 191 from Chicago to Los Angeles, crashed on takeoff with no survivors.

Denis Waitley never registered his complaint. In fact, he never returned his invalidated ticket for flight 191. He took it home and pinned it on a bulletin board in his office. In the wake of that experience, anytime he felt frustrated or got upset, all he had to do was glance at his ticket from flight 191. That ticket is a lifesymbol. It's an unforgettable reminder that life is a gift that should not be taken for granted.

After performing the funeral for Hilma and hearing that story about Denis Waitley, I became intentional about identifying and accumulating my own lifesymbols. My life is a story, a story that God is writing through me. It's His-story. And I need to identify the story lines that the Author of my faith is scripting for me. Lifesymbols mark the inciting incidents, the places where the plot thickens, the defining moments, and the beginning of new scenes. Lifesymbols are like cue cards that help us remember His script. They reveal who we're becoming by reminding us of where we've been and how we got here.

Alex Haley, the creator of the heralded miniseries *Roots,* is said to have had a picture in his office of a turtle sitting on a fence post. In Haley's words, "Anytime you see a turtle up on top of a fence post, you know he had some help." That picture was Haley's way of reminding himself of how he got to where he was. He had some help! I wonder if having Goliath's armor served the same function for David. The sheer size of the armor was evidence of the fact that David had some help. Goliath's armor was David's turtle on a fence post.

Memory Traces

By the end of his illustrious career as a neurosurgeon, Dr. Wilder Penfield had explored the brains of 1,132 living patients. Many of them suffered from epileptic seizures, and Dr. Penfield wanted to know why. Once the skulls were removed with the help of local anesthesia, patients were awakened so they could communicate with Dr. Penfield during the surgery. During some of these operations, Dr. Penfield made a fascinating discovery. Using mild electrical currents to stimulate different parts of the brain, Dr.

Penfield found that his patients experienced flashbacks. Vivid memories from the past replayed in their mind's eye, not unlike David's flashback to the lions and bears he killed when they attacked his flock.

One patient recalled every note from a symphony she had heard at a concert years before. The same spot was electrically stimulated thirty times, and each time she recalled every note. Another patient recalled sitting at a train stop as a child, and she could describe each train car as it went by in her mind's eye. Another patient visualized a childhood comb and was able to recount the exact number of teeth it had. Not only were the flashbacks extremely detailed, but in fact many of them predated the patient's first conscious memories.

Dr. Penfield concluded that every sight, every sound, every smell, every conscious thought, every subconscious dream is recorded on our internal hard drive, the region of the brain known as the cerebral cortex. Here is how it works. When you hear a song or see a picture or read a verse of Scripture, a line is traced on the surface of the cerebral cortex called a memory trace or engram. The brain functions like a deluxe Etch A Sketch. If you hear the same song or see the same picture or read the same verse of Scripture again, the line is retraced. With each repetition, the engram gets deeper and deeper until finally that song or picture or verse is engraved on the surface of the cerebral cortex.[2] It's also engraved on the soulprint.

Now let me add a caveat. Not all memories are created equal.

In fact, there are three kinds of memory. Sensory memory is as fleeting as a seven-digit phone number. Short-term memory has a little longer shelf life. You can recall what you wore, what you ate, and what you watched yesterday, but those details fade like an old photograph. Finally there is the holy grail of memory. A very small number of experiences make it into long-term memory. But it is those memories that shape your soulprint.

Generally speaking, the length of memory and how deeply an engram gets etched depend on the strength of the emotion tied to the event. So the stronger the emotion, the longer and stronger the memory.

Almost all of our long-term memories are associated with intense emotions, positive or negative. That's just the way God has wired us. Ninety-nine percent of our past experiences are quickly forgotten because they are barely felt. They may still be stored in the subconscious recesses of the cerebral cortex, but they are like computer files that can't be accessed because the software is outdated.

One dimension of stewardship is memory management. Like optimizing the hard drive on your computer, sometimes your memories need to be defragmented. Instead of keeping a record of wrongs, for example, certain memories need to be deleted. And you need to create a mental folder where you cut and paste the blessings of God. One way or the other, the process of self-discovery begins with a long look at old files. You have to inventory your memory.

AND SO LIFE IS

Alfred Adler is said to have begun counseling sessions with new clients with this simple yet revealing question: "What is your earliest memory?" And no matter how the patient answered, Adler would say, "And so life is." What he meant by that is this: our earliest memories are often our strongest memories in terms of impact on identity. For better or for worse, our earliest memories shape our soulprints in lifelong, life-changing ways.

One of my earliest and strongest memories is the first time I rode a bike. Part of the reason the memory is so strong is because I've heard my parents tell the story so many times. And that is one of the jobs of parents. They manage their children's memories by the stories they tell, the keepsakes they save, and the pictures they take. When I was four years old, I had a friend four houses down whose bike I borrowed on a daily basis. Then, one fateful day, he had the training wheels taken off. He marched down to our house and announced, "Now you can't ride my bike, because we took the training wheels off." I immediately marched down to his house, hopped on his bike, and rode it back to my house sans training wheels. If you want me to do something, don't tell me to do it. Tell me it can't be done! That dimension of my personality traces back to that early bike-riding memory. And so life is.

One of the most profound pieces of poetry ever written, "Germinal," was penned by an Irish poet named George Russell:

In ancient shadows and twilights
 Where childhood had stray'd
The world's great sorrows were born
 And its heroes were made.
In the lost boyhood of Judas
 Christ was betray'd.[3]

Judas didn't just decide as an adult to betray Christ. The seeds of betrayal were planted in the soil of his youth. That certainly doesn't excuse what Judas did, and he still could have decided not to do it. But choices have genealogies that often trace to our earliest memories.

According to the research of psychiatrist Emory Cowen, the level of popularity a child experiences in the third grade is the greatest predictor of mental health when that child becomes an adult. I find that fascinating, and I think it's true. It might not be the third grade. It could be second grade or fourth grade. But early experiences shape us in profound ways because children are like wet cement. If you had a great childhood, it's easy to read this paragraph. If you had a difficult childhood, it's probably harder. But difficult childhoods have produced some of the strongest people I know, including King David.

David was a punching bag for his older brothers. In fact, they were still picking on him when he visited them in the Valley of Elah. His older brothers were the first giants in his life! And his own dad didn't see David's potential. When Samuel was lining up the sons of Jesse to anoint the next king, Jesse didn't even bother to call David. That had to hurt. But David didn't allow those difficulties to define him. Much like my bike-riding incident, I think David welcomed a challenge. He loved being underestimated. The less potential others saw in him, the more he wanted God to prove them wrong.

I don't know what difficulties you've endured, but they don't have to define you if you simply let them refine you. That's the choice: define or refine. And if you let them refine you, God will actually use those negative experiences to redefine you.

POSTIMAGINING

Leonardo da Vinci once made a distinction between two types of imagination: preimagining and postimagining. Preimagining is imagining the future before it happens. And that is what typically comes to mind when we think about imagination. We think of imagination in future-tense terms, but every parent of toddlers or teenagers knows that kids have imaginative memories too. Especially when they've done something they shouldn't have! Postimagining, for holy or unholy reasons, is reimagining the past after it happens. And it is a precious gift that we need to steward.

If you are a former athlete, you can identify with me when I say that the older I get, the better I was. As we get older, we tend to inflate how good we were or how hard it was. Memories are not objective. They are subjective, very subjective. And we have a tendency to romanticize or catastrophize the past to one degree or another. We all distort memories by minimizing some while magnifying others. And how we manage those past memories has a major bearing on how we view the future. Our memories can either empower us to live by faith or imprison us to live by fear. How we postimagine the past can make us or break us. And that's why it's so important to see the past through the eyes of God.

The older we get, the more important it is to manage our memories, simply because we have more of them. How we manage our memories will determine how we see life, how we see ourselves, and how we see the future. The importance of memory management cannot be overstated, yet most of us never give it a second thought. We've never evaluated our memories for accuracy. We've never reshuffled our memory decks to prioritize the good memories. And some of us have a very difficult time deleting the bad memories and emptying the mental trash.

We tend to think of stewardship in terms of time, talent, and treasure, but we've also got to be good stewards of the minds God has given us. And that includes our imaginations and postimaginations. Mismanaging our memories can be as debilitating as a mental handicap. The solution is postimagining the past in light of God's providence. Isn't that what the Psalms are? In them David is postimagining the experiences of his life and setting them to music. He is searching for reasons why. He is looking for providence in the midst of his pain. And, though we may not be songwriters who find catharsis via writing lyrics, we need to find a way to follow suit. And that's where lifesymbols come into play. Lifesymbols are all about seeing the purposes of God in our past experiences.

HINDSIGHT

God has gifted us with three kinds of sight: hindsight, insight, and foresight. That three-dimensional ability to look backward, look inward, and look forward is part of the image of God that sets us apart from the rest of creation. Animals are instinctual. While they have a modicum of memory, it is Pavlovian. They are reactive, not reflective. And even the hoarding of food, which seems like foresight, is nothing more than a hormonal response to shortening daylight hours.

Humankind, on the other hand, is metacognitive. And it's our ability to think about how we think that enables us to post-imagine the past. Life is lived forward, but it is relived backward. Part of discovering your soulprint is seeing the purposes of God in your past experiences. The past is not circumstantial. The past is providential.

We know that in all things God works for the good of those who love him, who have been called according to his purpose. For those God foreknew he also predestined to be conformed to the likeness of his Son.

When you view your past through the lens of Romans 8:28–29, you see that there is a plan being played out. It might not always make sense, but that's because we're not omniscient. We naturally view our present circumstances in the light of past experience. In other words, we live forward. But God starts with the end in mind and works backward. So, what is His ultimate end? We are predestined to be conformed to the image of Christ. That is the *immagine del cuore*. The ultimate objective of every circumstance is to cultivate the character of Christ in us. That's why the worst circumstances can double as the best circumstances, because they help us identify with the sufferings of Christ. And it's the life lessons we learn from the worst of circumstances that often make the best lifesymbols.

"Many lives have a mystical sense," observed Gulag survivor Alexandr Solzhenitsyn, "but not everyone reads it aright. More often than not it is given to us in cryptic form, and when we fail to decipher it, we despair because our lives seem meaningless. The secret of a great life is often a man's success in deciphering the mysterious symbols vouchsafed to him, understanding them, and so learning to walk in the true path."[4]

Those mysterious symbols must be turned into lifesymbols. And that starts with an inventory of the past. If you're willing to do some personal archaeology, you'll dig up some invaluable artifacts. Start by dividing your life into chapters, corresponding to ages and stages. Then go all the way back to your earliest memories. What are they? Positive or negative, how did they shape you? And how can God redeem those past experiences to help you move into your future destiny? Digging into your past can be emotionally exhausting, but remember, your destiny is hidden there. Pray for a spirit of revelation. Make sure you have a journal to record your thoughts. Start looking for those mysterious symbols that can be turned into lifesymbols. Then turn your wall or desk or mantel into an altar by finding a place to put them.

EXPLANATORY STYLE

In his book *Learned Optimism*, Dr. Martin Seligman says that each of us has what he calls an explanatory style. That explanatory style is the manner in which we explain to ourselves why things happen. And *why* is more important than *what*. It's not our experiences that make us or break us. It's our interpretation of and explanation for those experiences that ultimately determines who we become. Your explanations are more important than your experiences.

Let me give you an example. You go through a difficult divorce. And it's hard enough dealing with the present-tense realities, ranging from child custody to division of property, but then you have to deal with a plethora of past-tense memories. You not only have to explain the divorce to family and friends. You also have to explain it to yourself. And there are lots of options. You can explain it in terms of genetics: *Must be in the genes, because my parents got divorced too.* You can explain it in terms of incompatibilities: *We just weren't right for each other.* You can explain away your part of the problems and blame it on your ex: *He (or she) wouldn't or couldn't change.* Or you can assume too much responsibility and pin the blame on yourself: *It's all my fault.* The explanations are never ending. You can also overspiritualize or underspiritualize it. You can overanalyze or underanalyze it. You can overestimate or underestimate it. For better or for worse, there are lots of explanations for divorce. And the truth is, divorce is often complicated beyond our ability to decipher. But it's your explanations that will either empower you or debilitate you. They can be a catalyst for change or they can be as imprisoning as iron bars. And it's up to you. You can't change the past, but you can learn from it. And that's how you change the future.

There are lots of different explanations for the same experience. The tough part is choosing the right one. And that's where we need the holy hindsight to see the purposes of God in our pasts.

One of my heroes is Corrie ten Boom. During the Nazi occupation of Holland in World War II, the Ten Boom family risked their own safety by hiding Jews in their house. Then on February 28, 1944, their home was raided and Corrie and her family were sent to a concentration camp. Her father and sister died in the camps, but through a miraculous series of circumstances, Corrie survived. In 1975, her life story was made into a movie called *The Hiding Place*. And it was after watching that movie that I put my faith in Christ for the first time. For what it's worth, my newest lifesymbol is an old movie poster that I recently purchased. That framed poster of *The Hiding Place* frames my life. Every time I see it, I'm reminded of the night I asked Jesus into my heart.

For many years, Corrie ten Boom traveled the world sharing her experiences. Or maybe I should say, sharing her explanations for her experiences. Corrie would often speak with her head down. It looked like she was reading her notes, but she was working on a piece of needlepoint. Then, after telling her story of the atrocities she experienced at the hands of the Nazis, Corrie would reveal the needlepoint she'd been working on. She'd hold up the backside, which was just a jumble of colors and threads with no discernible pattern. And she'd say, "That's how we see our lives. Sometimes it makes no sense." Then she'd turn the needlepoint over to reveal the finished side. And Corrie would conclude by saying, "This is how God views your life, and someday we will have the privilege of seeing it from His point of view."

One of the great joys of heaven will be postimagining the past in light of eternity. The past will come into perfect perspective. Everything will make sense. And we'll no longer remember what we should forget and forget what we should remember. Our glorified bodies will include glorified minds. And our glorified minds will include glorified imaginations and postimaginations. What a moment that will be for those whose memories have been stolen by disease or injury! In a moment, they will remember who they are and who their loved ones are. And most significant, the faithfulness of God will be revealed in all its glory.

As Corrie concluded her talks, she would often recite a poem by an unknown author that explained the needlepoint in poetic terms. That poem doubled as Corrie's explanatory style.

My life is but a weaving between my God and me,
I do not choose the colors, He works so steadily,
Oft times He weaves in sorrow, and I in foolish pride,
Forget He sees the upper, and I the underside.

Not till the loom is silent, and the shuttles cease to fly
Will God unroll the canvas and explain the reason why.
The dark threads are as needful in the Weaver's skillful
* hand,*
As the threads of gold and silver in the pattern He has
* planned.*

Your soulprint is two-dimensional. Identity is the underside, and destiny is the upperside. Lifesymbols? They are the warp and woof. They are the threads that connect identity and destiny. They are the colors that mark defining moments. They are the frames that help us explain our experiences. They are the shuttles that refine us and define us. And if you will simply put yourself on the loom, God will weave a masterpiece.

The Crags of the Wild Goats

David was conscience-stricken for having cut off a corner of his robe.

—1 SAMUEL 24:5

was twenty-two years old. I was surrounded by pastors who had been in ministry longer than I had been alive. And I sat anxiously in my chair, bracing myself for a barrage of theological questions. It was the day of my ordination interview.

In all honesty, I secretly hoped they would ask me an eschatological question because I had just figured out when Jesus would return in the tribulation time line. I also thought I was on the verge of resolving the age-old tension between Calvinism and Arminianism. I was armed and ready for any and every question. Every question, that is, except the very first question posed by one of the pastors. It has since become one of my favorite questions because it's a great way to get a glimpse into someone's soulprint.

Here's the question: "If you had to describe yourself in one word, what would it be?"

I was expecting questions about the Bible. I wasn't expecting them to ask me about me. I understood the Bible. But me? No clue. Then a word came to mind, and I was pretty sure it would wow them. In fact, I wondered if my one-word answer would end the interview. I thought they might just give me my credentials on the spot without even checking references. My answer? "Driven."

I was so proud of my answer then. Not so much now. The

longer I lead, the more I realize how unsanctified and unhealthy my answer really was. This is embarrassing to admit, but my dream at that point in ministry was to pastor a thousand people by the time I turned thirty. Now, there is nothing wrong with church growth. In fact, no one wants to grow His church more than the One who originally established it. But I wanted the right thing for the wrong reasons. It was less about building His church and more about building my ego. It was less about His reputation and more about mine. Truth be told, I cared more about the numbers than the people.

The unholy drivenness I felt earlier in my career isn't unique to ministry. Every occupation has its ladder, and if you climb over people to climb the ladder, it'll be awfully lonely at the top. If you skip rungs, you may get to the top quicker, but you'll also be much more likely to fall. Without integrity, the ladder has nothing to lean against. Without integrity, you cannot fulfill your destiny, because your integrity *is* your destiny.

It's been more than fifteen years since that awkward interview, and I still wrestle with unsanctified motives. I'm as imperfect now as I was then, but I'm much better at recognizing and admitting my own imperfections. I've also learned a valuable lesson: what we think of as the goal isn't really the goal. The goal is *not* accomplishing the dream God has given to you. The dream is a secondary issue. The primary issue is *who you become in the process*. We fixate on *what* and *when* and *where*. God's primary concern is always *who*. And He won't get you where He wants you to go until you become who He wants you to be.

SEEK THE SHADOWS

Sometimes you have to die to the dream God has given you so that God can resurrect the dream in its glorified form. And by glorified form, I simply mean pursuing the dream for God's glory. When you stop living for selfish purposes, the pressure comes off. And that's when your destiny comes into focus.

We try so hard to manufacture opportunities, but anything that is manufactured by human effort doesn't come with God's warranty. We try so hard to impress people, but our attempts to impress are utterly unimpressive, aren't they? What's really impressive is someone who isn't trying to impress at all. Now, that's impressive. Our attempts to manufacture opportunities or impress people are the by-products of an unsanctified ego that wants to glorify self rather than die to self. And until we experience that death to self, we'll never come to life in the truest and fullest sense of the word.

During my driven years, I coveted speaking opportunities. I called the covetousness a calling, but I was the one trying to do everything within my power to manufacture those opportunities. I wanted to be on the stage. I wanted to be in the lights. But once again, I wanted it for the wrong reasons. And I had to allow Christ to crucify my covetousness over and over again. It wasn't until God sanctified my motives, and I stopped seeking opportunities, that those opportunities started seeking me.

I was recently speaking at a leadership conference, and I happened to be coupled with Louie Giglio for one of the sessions.

Louie is the founder of the Passion movement and pastor of Passion City Church in Atlanta. I got twelve minutes to speak. Louie got thirty minutes. In other words, we both got what we deserved. Louie is one of my favorite communicators, so I was excited about hearing him speak, but it is in a situation like this where your true motives are tested. If you're playing the comparison game, the better others do, the worse you look, and the worse they do, the better you look. As I sat there at the conference with Louie, I had a flashback to when I was a younger pastor full of insecurities and immaturities. I had mixed reactions to guest speakers. I wanted them to do well. After all, I was giving them our pulpit to preach in. But if I'm being completely honest, I didn't want them to do *too* well. Why? It might reflect poorly on me. And I don't want to be in someone else's shadow. I want the spotlight.

As Louie was speaking, I heard that still, small voice of the Spirit, and this is what I wrote in my conference notebook: "Seek the shadows." Like sunflowers that face east to soak in the morning sunlight, we crave the praise of people. We want every ounce of credit we think we deserve. But you don't get honor by seeking honor. You get honor by giving honor. Jesus said it this way: "Don't sit in the seat of honor."[1] But His challenge to His original disciples to sit in the lowest seat didn't keep them from asking the comparison question: "Who is the greatest among us?"[2] We want to know where we rank, but Jesus never pulled rank. And He challenges us to follow in His footsteps and wash feet. And that is what seeking the shadows is all about. You aren't looking for opportunities to get credit or get noticed. You're actually looking for opportunities to do things where you won't get credit or won't get noticed. That proves that you aren't living for the applause of people. You're living for the applause of nail-scarred hands.

Most of us wait to do something wrong until no one is watching, and we wait to do something right until someone *is* watching. That's not human nature. That is our sin nature. It's our unsanctified desire for self-glorification. This will seem counterintuitive, but you don't really care about people until you don't care what they think. Until you've been crucified to their opinions of you, you can't really help them the way you should. You have to die to them. And while you're at it, you might as well die to your agenda, your approval ratings, and your reputation.

One of my deepest desires is to be a better person in private than I am in public. I'm not there yet, but that is the goal. *I want those who know me best to respect me most.* That is the essence of integrity. And that test is never taken in the light. It's always taken in the shadows, just as David took it.

THE CRAGS OF THE WILD GOATS

Let me set the scene.

David is hiding out in the crags of the wild goats. For the record, that is precisely where I would have gone to hide out, simply because I would have wanted to say, "I'm going to the crags of the wild goats." It just feels manly saying it. *I'm going to the crags of the wild goats.*

David is a fugitive because his father-in-law, King Saul, is trying to kill him. And you thought you had in-law issues! The man who walked David's wife down the aisle is now hunting him down like a wild animal.

> *He came to the sheep pens along the way; a cave was there, and Saul went in to relieve himself. David and his men were far back in the cave. The men said, "This is the day the LORD spoke of when he said to you, 'I will give your enemy into your hands for you to deal with as you wish.'" Then David crept up unnoticed and cut off a corner of Saul's robe.*[3]

David and his band of brothers are deep within the crevices of the cave when Saul shows up. Then, in a comedic scene that would have the most catatonic Broadway critic rolling in the aisles, Saul goes into the cave to relieve himself. What he doesn't know is that David is in the stall next to him!

Now, this is where my seminary training comes in handy. This is where I dive into the original Hebrew language and ask questions like these: *What does the word* relieve *really mean? Are we talking number one or number two? What do the text and context suggest? What is the scholarly consensus on the point?*

Based on the amount of time spent in the cave, and leaning on personal experience, I think the evidence points to number two. Why? Because David has time to cut off a corner of Saul's robe! I don't think he would have time to make that maneuver if we're talking about number one. And I think this number one versus number two business has far more spiritual significance than we may realize.

If it had been number one, David would not have had much time to think about what he was going to do. If we're talking number two, however, his integrity is far more impressive. David had plenty of time to kill Saul. He didn't just resist a short-fused temptation. He had time to think about it and act on it. It had to feel like an eternity to David as he weighed his options. *Do I kill the king and assume the throne that rightfully belongs to me? Or do I risk missing the opportunity of a lifetime and keep living as a fugitive?*

The men who are with him certainly perceive it as a divine opportunity, but just because something looks like or feels like a God thing doesn't necessarily mean it's a God thing. Just because it's endorsed by your closest confidants doesn't mean it's a God thing. Just because it seems like a golden opportunity doesn't mean it's a God thing. *An opportunity isn't an opportunity if you have to compromise your integrity.* If you have to lie on a résumé or withhold information during an interview process, then it's not worth getting the job. If you get the job by compromising your integrity, then you'll keep compromising your integrity on the job. But if you are straight-up right from the get-go, then either your potential employer will respect you for it and hire you because of your integrity or they'll do you a favor and not hire you.

When National Community Church was just getting off the ground, we were presented with what seemed like a golden opportunity. Another church approached us about a possible merger.

The church was incredibly dysfunctional, with lots of internal issues, but they had twelve million dollars worth of facilities debt free. I thought we could handle a little dysfunction for twelve million, but I knew we would be doing it for all the wrong reasons. In order to seize that opportunity, we would have had to compromise our integrity. And when you compromise your integrity, what you're really compromising is the opportunity itself. In retrospect, I'm so glad we didn't move forward with the merger, because it would have destroyed our DNA as a church. It also would have destroyed our integrity. It was tough to walk away from a piece of property worth that kind of money, especially considering the fact that property on Capitol Hill was going for about ten million dollars an acre, but it was the right thing to do. The opportunity wasn't an opportunity, because it would have compromised our integrity as a church.

There are moments when every person's integrity is tested, and these are the most important tests you'll ever take. You'll be tempted to take the shortcut, but if you do, it'll short-circuit God's long-term plans for your life. Don't go there. Forfeit what looks like an opportunity for the sake of your integrity.

David is a few inches and a few moments away from becoming king of Israel. All he has to do is stab Saul in the back. This situation seems like a God-ordained opportunity, but you cannot judge the will of God by the uniqueness of the circumstances. And the ends never justify the means. David knows that Saul was anointed and appointed by God. It is against the law to kill the king. God is the one who put Saul in, and God is the one who can take him out. David refuses to take matters into his own hands, because then his fingerprints will be all over it. And when we get our fingerprints all over something, it usually means we are taking matters into our own hands instead of putting them into the hands of Almighty God.

When I look back at the defining moments in my life and dust for prints, the greatest moments are the moments when my fingerprints are nowhere to be seen. All I see are the fingerprints of God.

EPIC INTEGRITY

David was conscience-stricken for having cut off a corner of [Saul's] robe. He said to his men, "The LORD forbid that I should do such a thing to my master, the LORD's anointed, or lift my hand against him; for he is the anointed of the LORD." With these words David rebuked his men and did not allow them to attack Saul.[4]

David sneaks up and cuts off a corner of Saul's robe. Impressive, isn't it? I don't know about you, but I tend to have heightened awareness when I'm in the bathroom. It's no small accomplishment to sneak up on someone else when he is in the stall. And while we're at it, props to David's entire band of brothers. If I know anything about the male gender, I know that men never outgrow potty humor. How they didn't bust out laughing as Saul made kingly noises is next to miraculous. How they remained silent, not a single giggle, is one of the great unsolved mysteries of Scripture.

This was quite a feat. I'd be patting myself on the back, but David is beating himself up. He is conscience stricken. Seriously? Saul is trying to assassinate you, and your conscience is bothering you because you cut off a corner of his robe?

David is a battle-hardened warrior at this point, but his conscience is still sensitized to the conviction of the Holy Spirit. The injustices David has experienced haven't desensitized him. They have actually softened his heart and fine-tuned his conscience. And it's a fine-tuned conscience that not only keeps us from doing what is wrong but also prompts us to do what is right. There is an old adage: "Let your conscience be your guide." Like spiritual GPS, the conscience prompts us to make U-turns when we do something wrong. But it also prompts us to make right—or righteous—turns. A fine-tuned conscience guides us to our destinies like the GPS voice that notifies us of our next turn.

In my mind, David could have easily justified killing the king. After all, it could have qualified as self-defense, especially if David were appointing the judges. But if David had killed Saul while Saul was relieving himself, I think David would have been looking over his shoulder every time he went to relieve himself. After all, most kings who become king by killing the king who comes before them end up getting killed by the king who comes after them. And that is what happens when you compromise your integrity. You have to always look over your shoulder. Instead of being able to focus all your energy on looking ahead, you have to waste energy looking back. You can't focus on where you're going because you have to cover up where you've been.

This is a defining moment for David. It's a moment that will determine his destiny. It ranks right up there with defeating Goliath. Fighting Goliath took epic courage. Not killing Saul takes epic integrity. In fact, it may have been harder to not kill Saul than to kill Goliath. Killing Goliath was an act of power. Not killing Saul is an act of willpower. And willpower may be the purest form of power.

WILLPOWER

The New Testament makes a distinction between two types of power. *Dunamis* is the ability to do things beyond your natural ability. *Exousia* is the ability to *not* do things you have the ability to do. And the Cross is the ultimate example of this second kind of power. Scripture is explicit: no one took Jesus's life from Him. In John 10, He says four times that He is voluntarily sacrificing His life. "I have authority to lay it down and authority to take it up again."[5] The word "authority" is *exousia*.

I'm impressed with the *dunamis* of Jesus. He made the lame walk and the mute talk. He healed the sick and raised the dead. But I'm even more impressed with His *exousia*. It's not *what He could do* that changed my life. It's *what He could have done but chose not to* that changed me. As Jesus hung on the cross, He said, "Do you think I cannot call on my Father, and he will at once put at my disposal more than twelve legions of angels?"[6] Jesus could have escaped His suffering (and thereby aborted His redemptive mission) with one call for angelic backup.

A legion was the largest unit in the Roman military, consisting of approximately six thousand soldiers. So Jesus had around seventy-two thousand angels at His command. *One* angel would have done the trick! But Jesus refused to exercise *dunamis*. Instead, He chose to exercise His *exousia*. He let people mock Him. He let them spit on Him. He let them hit Him. He let them put a crown of thorns on His head. He let them nail Him to the cross. That's not just love. That's not just power. That's willpower. It wasn't the power of the Roman Empire that kept him on that cross. It was *exousia*. And that is the kind of willpower that was exercised by His ancestor David.

Resisting the temptation to take Saul's life was a defining decision for David. It almost seems like integrity was forcing him to miss an opportunity. It almost seems like integrity was robbing him of something that rightfully belonged to him, something he was anointed to do. But integrity refuses to take shortcuts—or maybe I should say, cut corners.

Integrity isn't sexy. It's not something that is celebrated in our culture. In fact, it almost seems like an endangered virtue. But integrity is the moral glue that holds all other virtues together. Without it in your life, everything falls apart. And that includes your destiny. You'll never fulfill your God-given destiny without integrity.

David faced an integrity test in this story and passed with flying colors. He didn't need to take matters into his own hands. He needed to prove that he wouldn't take matters into his own hands.

He needed to prove to God that he could be trusted in the cave. After all, if God can trust you to do the right thing when Saul is on the throne, then He can trust you to do the right thing when you're sitting on the throne.

One definition of integrity is *doing the right thing even when no one is watching*. Well, no one was watching. David was in a cave in the middle of nowhere. You can't get much farther away from civilization than the crags of the wild goats. And I think that added to the temptation, because the farther away you are from home, the harder it is to keep your integrity intact. That is why business trips and travel to foreign countries and the transition to college can be so dangerous. You feel less accountable, because you feel more invisible. And it is that false sense of invisibility that makes you more susceptible to sin. I can think of half a dozen ways that David could have killed Saul and covered it up. No one had to know. No one had to see. But David knew the All-Seeing Eye was watching him.

THE UMBRELLA OF AUTHORITY

I have not sinned against you, even though you have been hunting for me to kill me.

May the LORD judge between us. Perhaps the LORD will punish you for what you are trying to do to me, but I will never harm you.… May the LORD therefore judge which of us is right and punish the guilty one. He is my advocate, and he will rescue me from your power!

When you violate your conscience, you put your own reputation at risk. You also have to become your own advocate, because you have stepped outside the boundaries of God's will. But when you obey God by living within the guardrails of a conscience that is fine-tuned to the Holy Spirit and Holy Scripture, then it's God's reputation that is at risk. As David experienced, God becomes your advocate. So the real issue when it comes to obedience is this: do you want to be your own advocate, or do you want the Almighty advocating for you?

When we submit our lives to God's authority by living with integrity, then we come under His umbrella of authority. And that umbrella of authority shelters us and provides us with a supernatural covering. It also takes all the pressure off us.

There are those who believe that tithing would add financial pressure to their lives by taking away 10 percent of their income. It's not true. Tithing relieves financial pressure because you are no longer responsible for your finances. God is. And God can do more with 90 percent than you can do with 100 percent. As an act of integrity, tithing forms a supernatural covering over our finances. Ultimately, the only thing we ought to fear is living outside the umbrella of His authority. Nothing fills you with holy confidence like knowing that God Himself is your advocate. You don't have to take matters into your own hands, because they are in the hands of God Almighty. You can bless those who curse you. You can pray for those who persecute you. You can love your enemies. Why? Simply because you know that God is your advocate.

I know lots of people who don't like their bosses. And for some, the dislike is warranted. But when you allow a seed of bitterness to take root in your spirit, you don't leave your boss at the office. You take him home with you. You take him on vacation with you. He's not just your boss at work. He becomes your boss everywhere all the time. We waste far too much emotional energy allowing others to control us in unhealthy and unholy ways. How? By treating them the way they treat us. But David refuses to go down to Saul's level. That's integrity. It doesn't allow others' actions to control one's own reactions, which is situational ethics at its worst. Integrity is making the right decision no matter when, no matter where, no matter what. If David had killed Saul, Saul would have been his king forever.

Can I remind you that your boss doesn't control you? Neither does your spouse or friend or professor or coach or roommate or colleague. *You control you.* I don't care if your boss is hunting you down like a wild animal trying to kill you. You still control you. Don't lie because others lie. Don't gossip because they gossip. Don't cheat because they cheat. Don't get negative because they get negative. Don't downgrade your integrity to the level of the people around you. Try to upgrade the people around you. If you refuse to compromise your integrity, you have a shot at earning the respect of the people you work with. And that is what David does. Here's what Saul said to David:

> *You are a better man than I am, for you have repaid me*
> *good for evil.... May the LORD reward you well for the*

kindness you have shown me today. And now I realize that you are surely going to be king, and that the kingdom of Israel will flourish under your rule.[8]

The Bible is full of stories about people who refused to compromise their integrity in tough workplace environments. And it was often their unwillingness to compromise that set the stage for miracles. If Shadrach, Meshach, and Abednego had compromised their integrity by bowing to the ninety-foot idol, they would have never been delivered from the fiery furnace because they would not have been thrown into it in the first place. It seems as if keeping their integrity intact was a dangerous thing to do, but it's always the exact opposite. It's dangerous compromising your integrity, because you don't allow the Advocate to intervene on your behalf. It was Shadrach, Meshach, and Abednego's integrity that led to the fourth man, the Son of Man, delivering them from the flames. And my favorite part of the story? "Not a hair on their heads was singed, and their clothing was not scorched. They didn't even smell of smoke!"[9] Integrity won't keep you from getting thrown into a fiery furnace, but it will keep you from smelling like smoke. And it won't just protect you. It will also convict the people around you. Nebuchadnezzar repented when he witnessed the uncompromising integrity of the Jewish trifecta. Saul did the same in response to David's act of epic integrity.

If you want to fulfill your destiny, don't compromise your integrity. Or in the context of David's story, *don't cut corners*. It's that simple. It's the little compromises that lead to major problems. If you cut corners, it may seem like you are seizing an opportunity, but you are actually compromising it, because any time you compromise your integrity, you compromise the opportunity.

INTEGRITY TESTS

As this chapter moves toward its end, I realize that you might feel like you've already failed the integrity test. The truth is, we all have. But the good news is that God allows us to retake the tests we have failed. Failure is never final as long as we seek forgiveness. And sometimes our failed tests teach us invaluable lessons we couldn't learn any other way.

A few years ago I failed an integrity test. I was speaking at a community meeting on Capitol Hill, giving an update on the coffeehouse we were building. The community was suspicious of a church building a coffeehouse, so I was trying to be as politically correct as possible. At the end of my briefing, I fielded questions, and someone asked me the meaning of the name of the coffeehouse. The name, Ebenezers, is taken from 1 Samuel 7:12 and means "Hitherto the LORD has helped us." We named it that because there were so many Ebenezer moments during the zoning process when God miraculously intervened on our behalf. But instead of glorifying God by sharing the literal meaning, I paraphrased. And that paraphrase was a compromise that pricked my conscience. I said it meant "So far, so good," but the second I said it, I knew that I had grieved the Holy Spirit. That isn't what it means, because that takes God out of the equation!

Now let me put the situation in context. A few weeks before this meeting, we had hosted our annual Easter Eggstravaganza on Capitol Hill. And while we blessed thousands of people that day, one guest complained. She said we talked about Jesus too much. God forbid! We are a church, after all, and it was Easter! But nothing would pacify her antagonism toward us. Well, that woman was at that community meeting, and it put me on the defensive. So instead of offending this woman, I offended the Holy Spirit.

After the meeting, my conscience agonized over that sin, and I apologized to God. I knew I had failed an integrity test, and I asked God for a second chance. Over the years He's provided plenty of opportunities to take that test over again. And I've passed those tests, in part because of the earlier failed test. In the wake of that experience, I promised God that I would never again take Him out of the equation. I promised that I wouldn't be defensive about my relationship with my advocate. And I promised that I would unapologetically and unashamedly give God the glory any time I had the opportunity to do so.

I also came up with a personal translation of 1 Samuel 7:12. I decided to tweak the old adage "So far, so good" by taking "good" out of the equation. My translation? "So far, so God." That verse, 1 Samuel 7:12, and that mantra, initialized as SFSG, are inscribed on our coffee-cup sleeves at Ebenezers. And if someone is offended by that, so be it. At least God isn't offended!

One of the most important decisions you'll ever make is who to offend. Trust me, you'll offend somebody. But make sure that somebody isn't the Almighty! I'm guessing that David's compadres were offended when David didn't kill Saul. He didn't heed their advice. And frankly, they were sick and tired of hiding out in caves. I'm sure they second-guessed their leader, but David wasn't afraid of offending them. David was afraid of offending God. And that holy fear isn't just the beginning of wisdom; it's also the beginning of integrity. The fear of God is the sign of a fine-tuned conscience. But over time, the desire to do what is right in the eyes of the Lord is motivated by more than the fearful fact that God sees us when we do something wrong. It's motivated by the fact that He sees us when we do something right. The desire to do what is right in the eyes of the Lord is motivated by the fact that we are the apple of His eye. So integrity begins with the fear of God, but it ends with love for God.

MONUMENT TO SELF

David was more concerned about offending God than offending his friends because he cared more about God's reputation than his own. And to really appreciate this dimension of integrity, all you have to do is compare David with Saul. Saul was more concerned about his own reputation than God's reputation, and that single differentiating factor is why their destinies diverged. Saul may rank as the most insecure leader in Scripture. And that insecurity didn't just erode his integrity. It also derailed his destiny. Two verses double as two defining moments in his downfall.

Saul built an altar to the LORD; it was the first of the altars he built to the LORD.[10]

So far, so God. Saul is giving credit where credit is due. He is acknowledging that God is the One winning the victories. But all that changes in just a chapter.

Saul went to the town of Carmel to set up a monument to himself.[11]

Somewhere between 1 Samuel 14:35 and 1 Samuel 15:12, Saul stopped building altars to God and started building monuments to himself. And the prophet Samuel sees right through the smoke screen, asking him, "Although you were once small in your own eyes, did you not become the head of the tribes of Israel?"[12] Who build monuments to themselves? It's those who think little of themselves. Pride is a by-product of insecurity. So the more insecure you are, the more monuments you need to build.

Now let me ask a tough question that demands an honest answer: are you building altars to God or monuments to yourself? Whose reputation are you more concerned about: your reputation or God's reputation? If you care more about your own reputation, then you are building monuments to yourself, and your relationship with God is self-serving. You aren't really serving His purposes. You are practicing a selfish spirituality that wants God to serve your purposes. And there is a name for that: *idolatry.* If you

aren't careful, your God-given dream can become more important to you than the Dream Giver Himself. God is no longer the
be-all and end-all. He becomes the means to a lesser end. And that
is when the dream God has given you to glorify Him becomes an
idol that robs Him of the glory He deserves. If David had killed
Saul to assume the throne, the throne would have become an idol
in his life. He was the rightful heir to the throne by virtue of his
anointing, but that doesn't excuse compromise. It was David's
willingness to give up the throne that proved to God he was ready
to sit on it.

For Saul, the downfall began when he started comparing
himself to David. And when you play the comparison game, no
one wins! It results in either pride or jealousy, and both of them
will cause you to compromise your integrity. For Saul, it was jealousy. Instead of keeping his eyes on God, he kept a jealous eye on
David.[13] And therein lies the great irony in this story. David was
Saul's greatest asset. He helped Saul save face against Goliath. He
secured Saul's kingdom against the Philistines. He even played
music on his harp to soothe Saul's soul. Saul should have been
singing David's praises, but when you're insecure, your greatest
asset becomes your greatest threat. Comparison will sabotage
your destiny by undermining your integrity.

My friend and mentor, Dick Foth, once told me about a deal
he struck with God: *If I don't take the credit, then I don't have to
take the blame.* What a great way to live and lead! And I can't help
but wonder if David struck the same deal.

Most of us spend most of our lives trying to prove ourselves to people, when all we have to do is prove ourselves to God. That is the key to your integrity and the key to your destiny. You don't have to prove yourself to people, because God is your almighty advocate. And if you live with integrity, then God will not only prove Himself to you; He will also prove you to others. The greatest freedom is realizing that you don't have to prove anything to anyone except God Himself. And that revelation is what made David a man after God's own heart.

Maybe it's time to quit taking the credit so you can quit taking the blame. Maybe it's time to quit proving yourself to people and start proving yourself to God. Maybe it's time to quit building monuments to self and start building altars to God.

Alter Ego

I will be humiliated in my own eyes.

—2 SAMUEL 6:22

can't dance. There, I said it.

I did the Riverdance for a variety show a few years ago. My sister-in-law tried to teach me the running man once. And if I concentrate really hard, I can pull off something resembling the electric slide. But my freestyle has no style. I'm rhythmically and choreographically challenged. And that's why it was such a traumatizing experience.

Our staff was in L.A. for a leadership conference. I held author and pastor Erwin McManus in high esteem, so we decided to visit the church he pastored. We walked in and found some seats up front. Big mistake. The services at Mosaic are highly interactive, and on this particular weekend they asked for a volunteer from the audience to do an interpretive dance. That is when my team turned on me. It was like the mutiny on the *Bounty*. They all raised their hands and volunteered me. *Mortified* isn't a strong enough word for what I felt. I couldn't say no without creating a scene, so I reluctantly crawled up on stage. It wasn't the way I envisioned meeting Erwin. He told me I had sixty seconds to do an interpretive dance of chaos, and the music started playing. Ironically, that is the only kind of interpretive dance I could have pulled off. Trust me, it was chaos.

I was "dancing" on the outside, but I was dying on the inside. I died a thousand deaths in sixty seconds flat. I've never felt more self-conscious. I've never been more humiliated. And one of my mutinous teammates was thoughtful enough to capture "chaos" with his camcorder. If you listen carefully while watching the video, you can actually hear Erwin laughing in the background. Nice. Then, adding injury to insult, Mosaic's professional dancers followed my routine with a dance interpretation of love that was so beautiful and graceful that angels certainly wept. Real nice.

No one likes to be embarrassed. In fact, we do everything within our power to avoid embarrassment at all costs. But we need to be embarrassed for the same reason we need to fail: it keeps us humble. And humility is the key to fulfilling our destiny. The longer I live and lead, the more convinced I am of this simple truth: God doesn't do what God does *because* of us. God does what God does *in spite* of us. All we have to do is stay out of the way. And the way we stay out of the way is by staying humble. If we stay humble, there is nothing God cannot do in us and through us. And nothing expands our capacity for humility like embarrassment. If handled properly, a healthy dose of embarrassment is good for us. Embarrassing moments are like spiritual antioxidants. They purge the ego of prideful impurities. This I know from personal experience.

Embarrassing moments mark our lives in unique and powerful ways. Some of them cause us to cringe. Others make us chuckle. But one way or the other, they help us come to terms with who we are and, more significant, who we're not.

Most Embarrassing Moments

One of my earliest embarrassing moments that I can remember happened in the second grade. I fell in a mud puddle during recess, and my pants got soaked. The school nurse gave me a pair of checkered wool pants that smelled like mothballs. I'm pretty sure they were originally worn by a short hippie who donated them to the school in the late sixties after getting off drugs. He should have burned them. Not only did they look ridiculous, but my legs still itch. Honestly, I can't blame my friends for laughing at me. I'm pretty sure Jesus even chuckled.

One of my most embarrassing ministry moments happened a few years into our church plant. I invited a band to do a concert for National Community Church. We were a church of about a hundred people at that point, and I told the band that a hundred people would show up. I was still in the naive stage of leadership. Five minutes before the concert, the seven-member band was sitting in the green room envisioning a hundred people, and I knew that only four people were out there. I've never wanted the Rapture to happen so badly! I was praying Revelation 22:20: "Come, Lord Jesus." What ensued was one of the most awkward events I've ever been part of. There were more people in the band than in the audience. Part of me wondered if we should switch places. Give the band the auditorium so they would have more room and move the audience to the stage! To top it off, one of the four people in the audience, who was a worse dancer than I am, wouldn't stop dancing. It was so bad I'm pretty sure it qualified as sinful.

My most recent embarrassing moment? Listen, it's no fun getting a phone call at one o'clock in the afternoon asking you why you aren't at the wedding you're supposed to be officiating that was supposed to start at noon. I flat-out forgot. I was at the mall, in a dressing room, trying on clothes. I had to get home, shower, put on a suit, and drive forty-five minutes through a snowstorm to get there. I finally arrived at three o'clock. My ego never did show up.

Embarrassing moments are horrible, no doubt. But they are also wonderful. Few things are as freeing as a little embarrassment. It frees us from the burden of pretense, and it forces us to stop taking ourselves so seriously. In a sense, embarrassment is one way we die to self. And dying to self is one way we come to life.

The words *humor, humiliation,* and *humility* are all etymologically related. In fact, *humor* is a derivative of *humiliation.* One dimension of humility is the ability to laugh at ourselves, and I'm convinced that the happiest, healthiest, and holiest people on the planet are those who laugh at themselves the most.

Too many people live as if the purpose of life is to avoid embarrassment at all costs. They never put themselves in situations that might be awkward. So they forfeit joy. They never reveal who they really are. So they forfeit intimacy. They never take risks. So they forfeit opportunity. They try to avoid embarrassment at all cost, and the cost is their souls. Or should I say, their soulprints.

I'm not suggesting that you go out and embarrass yourself by doing something stupid. And I'm certainly not encouraging embarrassment that is the by-product of social cluelessness. But too often we allow the fear of embarrassment to get between us and

God. We're too embarrassed to share our faith or confront a friend or walk away from a sinful situation. But if embarrassment is the result of doing something right, it's holy embarrassment. And there are certain situations where embarrassment is the only way you can remain true to God and to yourself. It's either embarrassment or hypocrisy, embarrassment or sin, embarrassment or obedience. In those situations, embarrassment isn't something to be avoided. In fact, if we follow the example set by David, it is something to be cultivated and celebrated.

> *I will become even more undignified than this, and I will be humiliated in my own eyes.*[1]

POMP AND CIRCUMSTANCE

Let me set the scene.

It is David's crowning moment. He has defeated the Philistines. He has recaptured the fortress of Zion. He has been anointed the king of Israel. And now he's bringing the ark of the covenant back into Jerusalem. The energy is electric, and the expectations are ecstatic. Think ticker-tape parade in New York City on V-J Day, August 14, 1945.

Advisers have scripted every word, every move. Secret Service has secured every intersection. The parade route is marked and the crowds are controlled. Everything is going according to plan, and then David throws the plan out the window. No one saw it coming. In fact, no one wanted to see it, period. David begins to disrobe, and it's not a wardrobe malfunction. Mothers don't know whether to cover their children's eyes. His staff don't know whether to stop him. And a collective blush sweeps across the crowd. The king of Israel is down to a linen loincloth. Then His Majesty starts dancing like a little child without a care in the world. No inhibitions. Pure joy. It is like all the pain David endured while hiding out in the wilderness—all of the anger and grief and frustration—gets translated into this one cathartic dance. It is like the holy adrenaline from every victory he had won on the battlefield gets channeled into a clenched fist raised in celebration to the Lord. His gestures are awkward, but it's an authentic awkward. No one is sure what to think. No one is sure what to do. And that includes David's wife, Michal.

As the Ark of the LORD entered the City of David, Michal, the daughter of Saul, looked down from her window. When she saw King David leaping and dancing before the LORD, she was filled with contempt for him.[2]

I don't want to rain on your parade, but let me offer a warning. When you get excited about God, don't expect everybody to get excited about your excitement. Why? Your intensity confronts their passivity. When you completely yield yourself to God, it convicts the unconsecrated by disrupting their spiritual status quo. Some people will be inspired by what God is doing in your life, but others will mask their conviction with criticism. After all, it's much easier to criticize others than it is to change ourselves. Nine times out of ten, criticism is a defense mechanism for fragile egos. We criticize in others what we don't like about ourselves. And part of our soulprint dies in the process.

Michal isn't just critical. She's dripping with sarcasm.

> *When David returned home to bless his household, Michal daughter of Saul came out to meet him and said, "How the king of Israel has distinguished himself today, disrobing in the sight of the slave girls of his servants as any vulgar fellow would!"*
>
> *David said to Michal, "It was before the LORD, who chose me rather than your father or anyone from his house when he appointed me ruler over the LORD's people Israel—I will celebrate before the LORD. I will become even more undignified than this, and I will be humiliated in my own eyes. But by these slave girls you spoke of, I will be held in honor."[3]*

David was the newly crowned king of Israel, and this was his grand entrance into the capital city. It had all the pomp and circumstance of an Inauguration Day. And the significance of that is this: there was added pressure to act like a king. He had a reputation to protect. He had a crown to represent. If there were ever a moment when David would be tempted to act like a king, this was that moment. Kings don't disrobe and get jiggy with it. And no one knew that better than Michal. After all, she was King Saul's daughter. The princess grew up in the palace. She knew protocol. And this was *not* protocol. But David couldn't care less. His only care was making sure that God was celebrated like He could be and should be, even if it meant embarrassing himself in the process.

ROYAL ROBES

There is a powerful subplot in this scene, and it's one key to discovering your soulprint. The royal robes represent David's identity and security as the king of Israel. Like a priest's collar or an officer's uniform or a policeman's badge, the royal robes represent David's authority. Royal robes double as his status symbol.

Please don't miss or dismiss the significance of what David does. David doesn't find his identity or security in his royalty. David finds his true identity and true security as a worshiper of God Almighty. Disrobing symbolizes his naked humility before God. Disrobing symbolizes his naked dependence upon God. David doesn't find his identity and security as king. He finds his identity and security in the King of kings.

Discovering your soulprint always involves disrobing. You have to be stripped of the things you find your identity in. You have to let go of the things you find your security in. And it will feel like you are losing yourself in the process. But it is only in losing yourself that you truly find yourself.

So let me ask the question: what are your "royal robes"? Is there something you find your identity or security in outside your relationship with Christ? Is your identity based on who you are or *whose* you are? Is your identity based on what you can do for Christ, or is it based on what Christ has done for you? Do you find security in what you have? Or is your security solely found in the seal the Holy Spirit set on you when you submitted to the Lordship of Christ? Discovering your soulprint means finding your identity and security in Christ alone. He becomes your identity. He becomes your security. Nothing else. Nothing less. And the Cross becomes your only status symbol.

Disrobing means dying to self, and it begins with identifying the things we find our identity and security in outside a relationship with Christ. Now, here's the tricky thing: the idol is often something God has given us. After all, God is the one who anointed David king of Israel, so his royal robes were a gift from God. God gives each of us gifts too. But if we aren't careful, the gift can become more important than the One who gave it to us. That is when our gift becomes our idol. That is when the blessing becomes a curse. Why? Because we find our identity and security in the gift instead of the Gift Giver.

Be Yourself

I have a friend who pastored a thriving church for many years. Then he quit. When I asked him why, he said, "I wasn't able to be myself." What a tragedy. If there is any place where you should be able to be yourself, it ought to be the church. The church ought to be a place where we can confess our deepest doubts, worst sins, and wildest dreams. It ought to be a place where we can reveal who we really are—the good, the bad, and the ugly. Unfortunately, church is often a place where we act like everything is okay even though it isn't okay. And that lack of authenticity forces everyone to hide behind their royal robes. But what if it were a place where people had the courage to disrobe?

When I started out in ministry, I was trying to look like a pastor, act like a pastor, and be a pastor. Now I'm trying to be myself. And there is a big difference. Early on, I was more concerned with authority than authenticity. I've since experienced a paradigm shift. True authority derives from authenticity. One of my goals as a preacher is to reveal how human I am. I try to share my weaknesses and failures because I think it amplifies the goodness and greatness of God. And I've found that authenticity doesn't undermine my authority. The more authentic I am, the more authority I have.

As the pastor of a church that is comprised primarily of twenty-somethings, I'm more and more convinced that authenticity is what the next generation is looking for. They don't expect perfection, but they do expect authenticity. And if a leader has the courage to disrobe like David, it fosters a culture of authenticity. If leaders are transparent, it creates a culture of vulnerability. If leaders are not transparent, it creates a culture of secrecy. The Enemy wants us to keep our secrets because that is how he keeps us in solitary confinement. But if we have the courage to confess, we find that the greatest freedom is having nothing to hide. The fear of being found out is far worse than the embarrassment we'll feel when we confess our sins. In fact, a feeling of relief will quickly replace the embarrassment.

A few years ago, one of my spiritual heroes confessed a sin that shocked his congregation. At first I was disappointed. I didn't want to see him disrobed. But ultimately my respect for him grew stronger and deeper because of the way he handled his mistake. He owned it. He confessed it. And one by-product of the sin is that I felt closer to him simply because he became more vulnerable. My respect also grew deeper because he handled it with grace, God's grace.

David didn't hide behind his royal robes. He literally revealed himself. He wasn't trying to be a king. He was trying to be himself. And nothing takes more courage than that. There is an old adage: "If you is who you ain't, then you ain't who you is." Disrobing is the courage to reveal who we are and who we aren't. When we try to be all things to all people, we're trying to be God. We've got a Messiah complex. And if we try to be everything to everybody, we'll end up being nothing to nobody. At the end of the day, I'd rather be hated for who I am than loved for who I'm not.

ALTER EGO

A few years ago I was walking home from the office when a friendly neighbor said, "Hi, David." I don't know why, but I just said "Hi" back and kept on walking. For some reason, I didn't correct her by telling her that my name was really Mark. Later that week, the same scenario happened. And again I didn't have the heart to correct her. To make a long story short, she called me David for several years. At first it was sort of fun and funny. David was my alter ego.

Sometimes I'd walk by with friends and she'd call me David and we'd get a good laugh. Then, one day, I started getting nervous: *What if she comes to church and finds out who I really am?* And the fun was replaced with a burden of pretense. But I continued to pretend to be who I wasn't. After all, when someone has called you by the wrong name a hundred times without correction, it's not easy saying, "Oh, by the way, that isn't really my name."

The day of truth finally arrived. One day I was walking home when the neighbor who called me David was with some neighbors who knew my real name. I wanted to turn around or cross the street, but I kept going. The funeral march was playing in my head. As I got closer, I knew one of two things was going to happen. Either the other neighbors were going to say, "Hi, Mark," and she was going to give them a strange look. Or she was going to say, "Hi, David," and they were going to give her a strange look. Either way, they were going to give *me* a strange look. It was a no-win situation. For the record, it was the last time she called me David. In fact, I think it's the last time she said hi.

That is precisely what happens when we try to be who we're not: it's a no-win situation. At first it's fun having an alter ego. But the burden of pretense grows until we can't be ourselves anymore. We can't let down our guard. We can't relax our image. And we become trapped by the lie. We become the lie.

Many people's lives revolve around protecting and promoting their alter egos. Whether it's at home, at the office, or at church, their alter egos are their act. They pretend that everything is all right even when they are dying inside. They are always trying to impress people, even the people they don't like. And they are afraid of revealing their doubts or dreams or disappointments because it would imperil their alter egos that are supposed to be beyond reproach.

It takes tremendous courage to disrobe. In fact, it may be the rarest form of courage. Just as with Adam and Eve, our ancient instinct is to cover our nakedness with fig leaves. Nakedness is awkwardness. That's why emotional nakedness is so rare. And spiritual nakedness is even rarer. But isn't that what we secretly long for? And that is what the grace of God offers us. His atonement covers us with grace so that we don't have to cover ourselves with fig leaves. In the words of A. W. Tozer in *The Pursuit of God*, "The rest [God] offers is the rest of meekness, the blessed relief which comes when we accept ourselves for what we are and cease to pretend."

One reason why we love the Psalms is that in them David disrobes. It is naked poetry. David exposes his doubts. He strips down to his raw emotions: anger, lust, pride. There is no pretense in the Psalms. And that is what we should strive for.

IDENTITY ISSUES

Now let me drill a little deeper.

The way you see yourself is determined by what you base your identity on. And you have lots of choices. You can base your identity on how you look or who you know. You can base your identity on what you do or how much you make doing it. You can base your identity on titles or degrees. You can even base your identity on what you wear or what you drive. There are a million factors that form the composite of our self-concept, but all of us base our identities on something. And what we base our identities on will make us or break us spiritually.

Let me share a theory. It may seem counterintuitive at first, but I think it's true. *The more you have going for you, the more potential you have for identity issues.* Why? Because it's easier to base your identity on the wrong things. It's rather ironic, but the greatest blessings can become the greatest curses simply because they undermine our reliance upon God and become a source of pride. Instead of relying on God's grace, you rely on your brilliant mind or charming personality or good looks. Instead of living out the motto "In God We Trust," we trust the dollar bill that saying is inscribed on. Don't get me wrong: there is nothing wrong with money, smarts, charm, and all the rest. They are gifts from God. But if you fail to praise God for them, they become a source of pride. Pride is simply the failure to praise. And the lack of praise always gives rise to pride.

Long before the fall of Adam and Eve, there was the fall of Lucifer. It's one of the most ancient references in all of Scripture, but it's still our postmodern problem.

> *Your heart became proud*
> *on account of your beauty,*
> *and you corrupted your wisdom*
> *because of your splendor.*[4]

Who made Lucifer beautiful and wise? God did. So beauty and wisdom should have been a catalyst to worship the Creator. But instead of worshiping God, Lucifer wanted to be worshiped. That is the original sin. All suffering, all evil, all brokenness, all pain are the aftereffects of a chain reaction that can be traced all the way back to time before time, when Lucifer rebelled.

The Creator has hardwired you to worship. In fact, you can't not worship. The question is not whether you will worship. All of us worship all the time. The question is, *who* will you worship? And you have only two options: either you will worship God with a capital *G* or you will worship god with a lowercase *g*. And if you choose to worship the god of you, you'll become a disappointing little god to yourself and all who worship you. Ultimately, all identity problems are really worship problems. Identity issues are the result of worshiping the wrong thing.

David had a choice to make as he entered Jerusalem. He could absorb the adoration of the Jewish people and allow them to worship him as their newly anointed king, or he could chose to deflect their praise by disrobing. Disrobing was David's way of saying, "Let me show you who I really am." It was David's way of showing the people that he was just like them.

HOUSE OF CARDS

It's so easy to base your identity on the wrong things. And if you do, you're building a house of cards. Or to use biblical language, you're building your house on sand, and as Jesus said, you're set-ting yourself up for a great crash.[5]

The crash goes by a few different names. If you're in your twenties, it's called a quarter-life crisis. If you're approaching half-time, it's called a midlife crisis. And while it doesn't garner much attention, I think there is a fourth-quarter crisis right around the time of retirement. Here's what happens at each crisis: You base your identity on school and then you graduate. You base your identity on a job and then you retire. You base your identity on marriage and you get divorced. All of those things—school, job, marriage—are good things. But they make poor foundations on which to base your identity. You cannot find your security in them.

When I was growing up, my life revolved around basketball. I played two hours a day every day, and I got pretty good. In fact, I was a first-team All-American. Unfortunately, it wasn't the NCAA. It was the NCCAA. The extra *C* was for Christian. Basketball was a huge part of my identity, but the harsh reality is that the NBA doesn't do much recruiting at small Bible colleges. I waited by the phone on draft day, but they must've dialed the wrong number.

When my basketball career ended, part of me died—the part that based its identity on basketball. And that is what happens whenever we go through major life changes. As the foundation of our identity—the place where we felt secure—shifts, we lose our footing. That's why it's normal to feel a mixture of sadness and joy on your graduation day or wedding day or moving day or retirement day. You're beginning a new chapter of life, which is exciting, but there is also a loss in that gain. When you graduate from school, the student dies. When you turn twenty, the teenager dies. When you get married, the single person dies. When you retire, the vocation dies.

That's the downside. Here the upside: if you base your identity on Christ, you avoid the crises altogether. Your security is founded in the steadfast love of the Lord that never ceases. Your identity is found in the One who is the same yesterday, today, and forever. Jesus Christ becomes your cornerstone.

Desperate Measures

God couldn't care less about protocol. If He did, Jesus would have chosen the Pharisees as His disciples. God is looking for those who are so desperate for Him that they will go to ridiculous extremes to worship Him. Look at the people Jesus celebrates in the Gospels: fishermen who drop their nets to follow Him, a prostitute who crashes a party at a Pharisee's house, a disciple who jumps out of a boat and swims to shore when he sees Jesus, four friends who pull an ancient airlift and get their paralytic friend to Jesus in the most unconventional way, and a distinguished tax collector wearing a three-piece suit who climbs a sycamore tree just to get a glimpse of Jesus. That is who Jesus celebrates.

Religion is all about protocol. Following Jesus is all about desperation. It's all about a God who is desperate for us and a people who are desperate for Him. It's a desperation that is willing to fast for forty days. It's a desperation that is willing to give everything to the poor. It is a desperation that is willing to pray through the night. It is a desperation that is willing to endure crucifixion for the sake of reconciliation.

Desperate people take desperate measures. Isn't that what David does when he disrobes? David is overwhelmed. Wouldn't you be? The hopes and dreams of an entire nation rest on your shoulders. Imagine the pressure. David needs God. No, David is *desperate* for God. And that desperation leads to disrobing.

I grew up in a church tradition that called people to the altar for prayer if they had a need, and it was almost always an awkward experience. I always felt like people were wondering what was wrong with me as I walked to the altar. After all, it acknowledges guilt or need or doubt. And those are awkward things to acknowledge. But some of the greatest spiritual breakthroughs of my life have happened at the altar, and I think part of the reason why God used those altar moments is precisely because they were awkward. I never want to get to a place in my life where I'm not willing to look or feel or act awkwardly. I think awkwardness is a catalyst for spiritual growth. Are you willing to do things that feel awkward, like kneel at an altar or obey a crazy prompting of the Holy Spirit or have a tough conversation with a good friend? If you are, then God can use you!

Not long ago I spoke at a national gathering of pastors. It was a special honor because it's the fellowship I'm credentialed with. That night our general superintendent was preaching, and he invited us to the altar. I'm guessing there were ten thousand people in the audience. And part of me was tempted to stay put. After all, I was a speaker at the event. Then I felt a prompting of the Holy Spirit, and I knew I needed to obey it. The more God uses you, the easier it is to think that you're above or beyond putting yourself in awkward positions. But if you lose your raw dependence upon God, you lose His power and are left with just your own. I went forward that night and looked for the oldest pastor I could find. I covet the prayers of people who have been talking to Jesus for a long time. I'm not sure what came over me, but I started crying as he started praying. I felt so awkward. But that is how I knew it was right.

I'm at a place in my life and ministry where I crave awkwardness. I want to look awkward. I want to feel awkward. Why? Because it means I'm not settling for what is comfortable, what is acceptable. Let's not avoid awkwardness. Let's create it, cultivate it, and celebrate it.

I recently told our team at National Community Church (NCC) that we need to start doing more things that make people feel awkward. I know that doesn't sound seeker sensitive, so let me explain. Comfort impedes spiritual growth. Our attempts to create comfortable environments often produce immature disciples. My job is not just to comfort the afflicted. My job is to afflict the comfortable. Don't get me wrong: our goal as a church is to remove all sociological barriers that would keep people from considering the claims of Christ. If people are going to get offended, I want them to get offended by the Cross. I'm afraid that we don't even give people the opportunity to be offended by the Cross because we offend them before they can get there! So at NCC we work hard at creating environments that remove those sociological barriers. We want people to be able to sit in the shadows of our movie-theater campuses and investigate the gospel. But eventually they've got to come out of the shadows and into the light. In our efforts to create comfortable services, we do people a disservice. Breakthroughs happen as a result of awkwardness.

Have you ever felt prompted by the Holy Spirit to say something or do something that seems less than safe? Have you ever wrestled with the conviction of the Holy Spirit? Has the Spirit of God ever conceived in you something that seems crazy? The common denominator is always awkwardness. Doing the will of God is almost always accompanied by feelings of awkwardness, uneasiness, and unreadiness. You won't just feel like you're crazy. You'll probably look crazy to those who haven't heard what God said to you or felt what God conceived in you. Isn't that how David looked? His wife thought he'd lost his dignity. His staff thought he'd lost his mind. But that's when you need to swallow your pride. If you don't, your heart hardens and your soul suffers. If you do, that one small step will become one giant leap in the direction of your destiny.

AWKWARD MIRACLES

A few months ago we ended a service with an altar call. And it was awkward. We asked people who needed a miracle to come to the front of the theater, and everybody stayed in their seats. That lack of response is especially awkward when you're the one up-front waiting to pray for people. Then, as is typical, one person was brave enough to come forward, and lots of people followed in that one person's courageous wake.

I happened to pray with a woman named Renee who runs a missionary organization. I asked her what miracle she needed, and she told me about an orphanage in the Congo that her organization was trying to open. It would house sixty kids. But they needed fifteen thousand dollars to open the doors. I felt prompted not just to pray for her but also to take a spontaneous offering. More than five thousand was given at that one location that day, and when I shared the story the next week, another NCC location gave more than ten thousand dollars. In two weeks, we raised more than seventeen thousand dollars and gave sixty kids a roof over, and a pillow under, their heads. But here's what I want you to see: the miracle would not have happened if Renee had stayed in her seat. We wouldn't have done anything to help with the need because we wouldn't have known anything about it. But Renee's willingness to put herself in an awkward position translated into a miracle for those sixty kids in the Congo.

I'll never forget what Renee said to me on the way out of church: "You have no idea how hard it was for me to come forward." I told her I knew exactly how hard it was because I've been there and done that. It's awkward. But awkwardness is the only thing that stands between you and your miracle. And once you experience the miracle, you crave the awkwardness. You embrace it for what it is: holy embarrassment. And it's those awkward moments that will turn into defining moments, miraculous moments.

The only thing between you and your destiny is awkwardness. Are you ready to embrace it? Take off your royal robes, lose your alter ego, and step into your destiny by risking embarrassment. One more thing: don't forget to laugh at yourself along the way!

SCENE V

The Devil's Workshop

In the spring, at the time when kings go off to war, David sent Joab out with the king's men and the whole Israelite army.... But David remained in Jerusalem.

—2 SAMUEL 11:1

The Johari Window is a fascinating matrix on the study of human personality. I got my first peek through the window during a graduate course in psychology. Like a four-pane window, the four quadrants reveal four dimensions of one's identity. As you look through the different panes, you are taken to new places in self-discovery. Looking through the Johari Window is like seeing your soulprint from four different angles.

The first window, the arena quadrant, consists of those things *you know about you* and *others know about you*. This is who you are when everybody is looking. It is your public persona. It's what everybody sees and knows about you, but it is only the tip of the identity iceberg.

The next window, the facade quadrant, consists of those things *you know about you* but *others don't know about you*. This is who you are when nobody is looking. It's who you are after you get past the polite superficialities. Behind the facade are the deep disappointments you've never reconciled, the hidden dreams you've never verbalized, and the secret sins you've never come to grips with. This is the person you know you are, for better or for worse, but sometimes are afraid to reveal.

The third window, the blind-spot quadrant, consists of those things *others know about you* but *you don't know about you.* This is what others see in you but you cannot see in yourself. This is where you need prophets in your life who see the potential in you that you cannot see in yourself. This is also where you need true friends who have the courage to confront things in you that need to change. If you don't have someone who has permission to openly and honestly speak into your life, your blind spots will never be revealed.

The fourth and final window is the unknown quadrant, and it consists of those things *you don't know about you* and *others don't know about you.* This quadrant of your soulprint—your true identity before God—is made up of the things that are invisible to everyone except the All-Seeing Eye. And this is where the Holy Spirit plays such a vital role in your life. Until you see yourself through His eyes, you'll never get a vision of who you can become. The key to self-discovery is allowing the One who knit you together in your mother's womb to reveal things you do not and cannot know about yourself without His revelation. God knows you better than you know you, because He designed you, so if you want to get to know yourself, you've got to get to know God. In the words of C. S. Lewis in *Mere Christianity,* "Your real, new self…will not come as long as you are looking for it. It will come when you are looking for Him."

If you want to find yourself, you've got to look for God. Ignoring God is like ignoring yourself. You can ignore Him, but if you do, you'll always be a stranger to yourself. If, however, you have the courage to enter the unknown quadrant, you'll discover dimensions of your God-given identity and God-ordained destiny that have eluded you for your entire life.

Most people spend most of their time in the arena quadrant living for public consumption. Or they spend most of their energy in the facade quadrant pretending to be who they're not. The revelations and breakthroughs that can happen only in the third and fourth dimensions elude them. And they are content to live as strangers to themselves.

True freedom is found when you come out from behind the facade. And all it takes is honest self-examination. I can't promise that it won't be spiritually painful or emotionally exhausting. And you won't like everything that is revealed. But if you want to discover your soulprint, there is no other alternative. You've got to take a long, hard look at yourself through the third and fourth windows. And that is what David does with the help of a prophet named Nathan, who sees behind the royal facade.

IDLE EYES

Let me set the scene.

Like a retired athlete who misses game day or a retired politician who misses the campaign trail, David misses the battlefield. He misses the rush of adrenaline. He misses the camaraderie he felt in the camp. He misses making headlines in the next day's newspaper. David is no longer making history. David is history.

David is bored, and boredom is the seedbed of sin. We sin

because we have nothing better to do, literally. And the cure for sin is a vision from God. If you are consumed with a God-sized vision, you have less time or energy left over to sin. You're too busy serving God to sin against God. But if you're not busy serving God, you're more likely to sin against Him. As the old adage says: "Idle hands are the devil's workshop." So are idle eyes.

> In the spring, at the time when kings go off to war, David
> sent Joab out with the king's men and the whole Israelite
> army. They destroyed the Ammonites and besieged
> Rabbah. But David remained in Jerusalem.
>   One evening David got up from his bed and walked
> around on the roof of the palace. From the roof he saw a
> woman bathing. The woman was very beautiful, and
> David sent someone to find out about her.[1]

When the soldiers are away, the king will play. David's accountability structure is absent. His routine has changed. And the Enemy is painfully predictable in his temptation tactics. If we're not on the attack, playing offense for the kingdom, the Enemy will put us on the defensive by attacking us. David should be rallying the troops on the front lines. Instead, he's pacing the sidelines with very little to do except get in trouble. And that is when the Enemy is at his best and we're at our worst.

David is pacing his rooftop deck, dreaming of the glory of battles past. Then, out of the corner of his eye, Bathsheba catches his eye. As that image of a bathing Bathsheba passes through the optic nerve and into his visual cortex, David has a decision to make: look or look away. It's that simple. It's that difficult. His conscience—the same conscience that convicted him the day he cut off a corner of Saul's robe—tells him to look away. But David doesn't obey his conscience. And that is the moment temptation turns into sin.

It's hard to dissect sinful motivations, but I wonder if David is struggling with his masculinity. I wonder if his ego is suffering. I wonder if this is a midlife crisis. The warrior is no longer fighting battles or making headlines. And when a warrior stops making military conquests, there is a temptation to turn toward other conquests. When a warrior stops going to battle, how does he channel the testosterone that runs through his veins? When the warrior retires, in what does he find his identity? And the same kinds of crises are true regardless of gender or occupation. When we disengage from holy pursuits, we often reengage in sinful habits.

Sin comes in many varieties, but one of the primary strands is what I call a legitimate illegitimate sin. We attempt to meet a legitimate need, but we do it in an illegitimate way. We aren't patient enough to wait for God to meet the legitimate need in the legitimate way He has prescribed, so we look for a quick over-the-counter fix. And the legitimacy of the need makes the sin seem innocuous. We justify it with a selfish rationalization: *God wants us to be happy.* And He most certainly does. But anytime we take a sinful shortcut, we short-circuit true happiness. Sin may yield a moment of pleasure, but the side effect is always misery. And the misery is as enduring as the pleasure is fleeting. Sin is like selling your soulprint in a short sale. It's as foolish as Esau's selling his birthright to Jacob for a bowl of stew. It'll be your greatest regret at the end of your life because you'll have fallen short of fulfilling your true destiny. Sin is selling God and yourself short.

MORAL HONESTY

I am no longer surprised by sin. Not after all the confessions I've heard. I've counseled enough businessmen to know that just because you can manage a business doesn't mean you can manage yourself. I've prayed with enough politicians to know that just because you win a popular vote doesn't mean you like yourself. And I've talked, off the record, with enough pastors to know that just because you're ministering to others doesn't mean you're winning the sin battle yourself. Our potential for sin is exceeded only by our potential for self-deception. Sinful self-deception may be the only unlimited capacity we possess. So I'm no longer surprised by sin. What does surprise me is the person with the rare courage to confess. My opinion of people, when they confess their sins, never goes down. My opinion always goes up, simply because they are able to admit what the rest of us deny.

The process of sanctification undeniably results in fewer sins committed, but it's about more than sinning less. It's also about coming to terms with just how sinful we are. Sanctification results in a heightened awareness of the sinful motivations that infect the actions we take and the decisions we make. Too often we underestimate our sinfulness, thereby underestimating God's righteousness. And when we downplay sin, we downplay the grace of God.

David was a man after God's own heart. But that unique designation wasn't the by-product of moral perfection. Moral honesty is what made him a man after God's own heart. At first, David attempts a murderous cover-up of his illicit affair with Bathsheba. And that is his knee-jerk reaction to guilt. But after a God-ordained encounter with the prophet Nathan, David musters the courage to confess. And it's a very public confession. In fact, it may be the most publicized confession in history, having been read by millions of people over thousands of years. On the heels of his most grievous sin, David writes his most redemptive psalm. Psalm 51 takes us behind the facade quadrant and into the blind-spot quadrant. And the raw honesty is all too rare.

> I know my transgressions,
>   and my sin is always before me.
> Against you, you only, have I sinned
>   and done what is evil in your sight,
> so that you are proved right when you speak
>   and justified when you judge.
> Surely I was sinful at birth,
>   sinful from the time my mother conceived me.[2]

HOLY BEST

Remember the old nursery rhyme we learned as children?

Humpty Dumpty sat on a wall.
Humpty Dumpty had a great fall.
All the king's horses and all the king's men
Couldn't put Humpty together again.

All of us have felt like Humpty at one point or another. It feels as if our lives are falling to pieces and our hearts are broken beyond our ability to put them back together again. We feel helpless and hopeless. We don't even remember what the jigsaw puzzles of our lives are supposed to look like anymore. It's like we've lost the box top that reveals our soulprint. We forget who we are. We forget *whose* we are.

That's how David must have felt in the wake of his affair. At that point David is absolutely undone. His dignity is destroyed. His reputation is ruined. His heart is hardened. And he finally reaches the end of his spiritual rope. None of us like reaching the end of our rope. It's the scariest, weakest, and loneliest place we can find ourselves. But sometimes we have to reach the end of our rope before we will reach out for God. And that's when we discover a knot at the very end of the rope. That knot is the mercy of God. And it's the only thing that will stop a spiritual free fall.

In his memoir *The Sacred Journey,* Frederick Buechner wrote about his father's suicide when Frederick was a young boy. That experience shattered his soul, but through the painful process of recovery, he also discovered God's ability to mend the broken spirit. "When it comes to putting broken lives back together...the human best tends to be at odds with the holy best," observes Buechner. That distinction between "human best" and "holy best" is profound. Many of us never experience the "holy best" because we're trying to fix ourselves with our "human best" effort. But our human attempts to solve problems often further complicate them. We compound our problems. Buechner continues the thought: "To do for yourself the best that you have it in you to do—to grit your teeth and clench your fists in order to survive the world at its harshest and worst—is, by that very act, to be unable to let something be done for you and in you that is more wonderful still."[3]

We try so hard to fix our own brokenness, but there are problems beyond our ability to solve, hurts beyond our ability to heal, and memories beyond our ability to forget. What do we do with those? How do we get out of the prison of past pain? How do we overcome the regrets that haunt us? The only way out is through allowing God to reconstruct our minds, our hearts, and our spirits. And that is God's specialty.

"When I invited Jesus in my life," said C. S. Lewis, "I thought he was going to put up some wallpaper and hang a few pictures. But he started knocking out walls and adding on rooms. I said, 'I was expecting a nice cottage.' But He said, 'I'm making a palace in which to live.'"[4]

King David didn't just live in a palace. He was a palace. And so are you. You are God's palace, God's temple. And He wants to dwell in you. But that requires major renovation. And it often starts with demolition. God needs to tear down the facade so He can re-lay the foundation.

That's what God has done in my life over recent weeks. For the first time in my pastoral ministry, I took a sabbatical. I wish I could say it was a time of refreshing, but it was anything but. It was emotionally exhausting. I feel like God took me behind the woodshed. He revealed some things I didn't want to see but couldn't afford to ignore.

Laying down my identity as a pastor helped me see myself for myself. And I didn't like everything I saw. The need to be needed is so deeply entrenched in my heart that it was hard to disengage. Some subtle sins still rear their ugly heads in ways that are almost imperceptible. And bad habits I thought I buried long ago seem to have nine lives. To be blunt, my sabbatical was spiritually painful. I saw how fragile my ego is. It revealed how out of whack my priorities are. And I felt overwhelmed by the issues I need to address. When my sabbatical came to an end, I came to one conclusion: I can't fix myself. I need God to save me from myself.

That is where David found himself in the wake of his affair. He couldn't fix himself. And that can be a terrifying place to be. But it often proves to be a turning point in a person's life. Sometimes God cannot or will not put our lives back together until they have fallen apart.

Psalm 51 is used daily in Jewish prayer liturgies. But one verse

in particular, verse 17, is repeated three times a day as a prelude to
silent prayer. It reminds us of not only our brokenness but also of
God's holiness.

> The sacrifices of God are a broken spirit;
> a broken and contrite heart,
> O God, you will not despise.

Instead of trying to fix your brokenness, maybe you need to
embrace it. Your brokenness may be a blessing in disguise. Like a
mother who is drawn to her crying baby, God is drawn to human
brokenness. And if you allow Him to, He will put you back together in ways that will one day cause you to celebrate the brokenness as a gift from God. It's in our brokenness that God's holiness
is most clearly revealed.

PURE GENIUS

God also uses our brokenness to reveal to us our soulprint. Our
destiny is often revealed in our own misery and failure. That may
not be how or where we want to discover our destiny. But it's in
working through our own tragedies, our own pain, and our own
problems that we're able to help other people with their tragedies,
their pain, and their problems.

"Where a man's wound is," observed Robert Bly in his book
Iron John, "that is where his genius will be." That is certainly true
of David. The Psalms are pure genius. But their genius is the by-

product of David's pain. The greatest psalms came out of the most painful experiences in his life.

Over the past three decades, Mothers Against Drunk Driving has raised awareness, pushed legislation, and recruited more than three million members in its noble cause to stop drunk driving. It's impossible to calculate the number of lives they have saved, but MADD has made a difference. What you might not know is that the genesis of their lifesaving mission traces back to a tragic death. The founder, Candy Lightner, lost her thirteen-year-old daughter to a drunk driver. She could have wallowed in her personal pain. She could have drowned in the anger she felt toward the driver who took her daughter's life. But instead of getting mad, she formed MADD. She redeemed the pain and discovered her destiny.

For Candy Lightner, forming an organization was the way she redeemed her pain. For David, it was writing songs. Songwriting was a form of catharsis; it's the way David dealt with what he had done. His lyrics are like an autopsy on guilt and doubt and anger. The Psalms contain lots of genres of music. Some psalms read like beautiful ballads to the Creator. Other psalms, including Psalm 51, are definitely soul music.

Sometimes our destiny is revealed via beautiful moments that cause joy. Other times, our destiny is revealed via broken moments that rob joy. For David, this is one of those moments when all joy is gone. David is begging God to restore the joy that guilt has stolen. And out of the depths of his soul comes a guttural song. From the bottom of his heart, at the top of his lungs, David sings,

"Give me back my joy again."[5] And he sings it over and over again like a chorus.

Maybe you are there. Joy seems lost. And you're not even sure how you got there. Let me remind you of this simple truth: you are not alone. You have a High Priest who feels your pain. In fact, your pain hurts Him more than it hurts you. And if you are a parent, you know that is more than a platitude. All I can say is this: give it time. Most problems don't happen overnight, and they don't go away overnight either. But give it time, and God will restore your joy. And that joy will be yours for eternity. In the meantime, you need to embrace your brokenness. This is difficult to write, and even more difficult to read, but there is a potential ministry in your pain. You've got to redeem the pain and turn it into someone else's gain. That is how wounds are healed. That is how destinies are revealed.

Like a good shepherd who breaks the leg of a lamb that has a tendency to stray away from the flock, thereby putting itself in danger, God breaks us when and where we need to be broken. It seems like cruel and unusual punishment, but it is God's way of protecting us from ourselves. And the breaking always has a redemptive purpose. The hurt will heal stronger. And God graciously carries us on His shoulders until we have the strength to stand on our own two feet again.

Are there any strongholds in your life? Lust? Anger? Pride? Until those strongholds are broken, you cannot fulfill your destiny. So the question is this: are you willing to submit to short-term pain for long-term gain?

Most of our prayers revolve around God's changing our circumstances, but God doesn't always want to change our circumstances. He wants to use those circumstances to change us! And it starts with breaking the strongholds in our lives. The good news is that God always heals what He breaks. And much as with the human body's natural healing properties, the broken spirit will be stronger after the break than it was before.

The average adult has 206 bones. And those bones are constantly going through a biological process called remodeling. The bones are always being broken down and built back up. Osteoclasts break down the bone, and osteoblasts rebuild them. It is that same process of remodeling that the spirit goes through after repentance. And just like bones that are stronger after a break than they were before, so the spirit is strengthened. Our spirits are constantly going through this process of remodeling. And if we submit to the breaking process, we will eventually be strongest in those places where we have been broken. But in order to heal, we need to go through the same process of self-examination that David did in Psalm 51.

DEFENSE MECHANISMS

I don't know about you, but I'm not a huge fan of exams. It doesn't matter whether they're academic or medical; I find them stressful. My blood pressure goes up simply because someone is checking my blood pressure! The reason I don't like exams is because they reveal what I don't know or don't want to know. But

I've come to terms with the fact that, while I may not like them, I need them. The only alternative is ignorance. And ignorance is not bliss.

When my dad recently had his annual exam, the doctor discovered melanoma. No one wants to make that discovery, but what's the alternative? If you don't find out what's wrong, then you can't make it right. The problem will only get worse if it remains undiscovered. If skin cancer goes undetected, it can get into the bloodstream and spread throughout the body. What is true physically is also true spiritually. If we turn a blind eye to our sin, it doesn't go away. It goes from bad to worse. You cannot heal from it until you diagnose it.

Our culture isn't very adept at self-examination. We'd rather watch reality TV and live vicariously through others. Maybe that's why many of us know more about our favorite celebrities than we know about ourselves. It's so much easier obsessing over others than it is working on ourselves. And that's why so many of us are strangers to ourselves. We hardly know who we are. And the only solution to superficiality is self-examination. You've got to take a long, hard look in the mirror.

Sometimes the mirror is a prophet in our lives. It takes someone with supernatural insight to see our blind spots. We need someone who is honest enough and courageous enough to confront us. In David's case, the prophet needed an even greater measure of courage because David was the king, and kings often kill prophets who say what kings don't want to hear. The prophet Nathan must have prayed for the right words, and he definitely found them. He spoke in terms that took David back several decades. He told the former shepherd a story about a rich man who took a lamb from a poor man. Instead of a frontal attack, Nathan got past David's defenses by telling a story. And there's nothing like a story to get past a person's defenses and sneak in the back door.

So David got mad at the rich man who stole the poor man's only lamb. And that's when Nathan delivered the punch line. Remember the manly greeting that was popularized a decade ago: "You da man"? That manly compliment might find its origin with Nathan. But in David's case, it was an indictment: *You da man.* Nathan helped David see his own sin by getting him to look through the third windowpane: the blind-spot quadrant. That is what prophets do. And that confrontation often leads to confession.

All of us need those who have the freedom to speak into our lives, the freedom to say what we don't want to hear, the freedom to call us on the carpet. Each of us needs a Nathan. And there are moments when we need to be Nathans.

When you look back on your life, who do you respect the most? My guess is that there are people in your past who pointed out a blind spot or two. They saw past the facade. They confronted a sin. They said something you didn't want to hear. And you hated them for it then, but you respect them for it now. At the end of our lives, we'll have lost respect for those who simply said what we wanted to hear. The people who will have earned our respect are the prophets who had the courage to risk the relationship by saying things we didn't want to hear.

PERSONAL PROPHECIES

According to Laurie Beth Jones, 40 percent of our lives are based on personal prophecies. And while that percentage cannot be proven precisely, I think there is tremendous truth behind the statement. We need prophets who speak into our lives, their words altering the trajectories of our lives. In her book *The Power of Positive Prophecy,* Jones tells a story about a man named Michael:

> *I grew up in an alcoholic household where I never heard a positive word. On my way home from school I would always stop in at Jimmy's, the local dry cleaner, because he kept candy on the counter. He got to know me, and told me one afternoon, "Michael, you are a very smart boy. Someday you are going to run a very big business." I would listen to him in disbelief and return home only to get called a "dog" and knocked around by my dad. But you know… Jimmy the dry cleaner was the only person I can remember believing in me…. Today I run a multimillion-dollar health care organization, just like Jimmy predicted. I guess you could say that a dry cleaner was the prophet in my life.*[6]

You may not see yourself as a prophet, but you are one. You're a prophet to your friends. You're a prophet to your children. You're a prophet at work and a prophet at home. And your words have the potential to change lives by helping people discover their identities and destinies.

We have a mistaken notion that prophets form a very small, very select group of individuals. Not true. Moses said, "I wish that all the LORD's people were prophets."[7] That is a categorical statement. And it has changed the way I see our church. I don't see people as parishioners. I see every single person as a potential prophet. Jewish philosophers believed that becoming prophetic was the crowning point of mental and spiritual development. It wasn't an exception. It was an expectation. The more you grow, the more prophetic you become.

Over the past year, I've asked God for more prophetic insight. I'm tired of shallow conversations with no eternal consequence. I want to have conversations that punctuate a person's life in ways that will change his or her destiny. And while I still engage in small talk, I've had far more conversations that have proven to be defining moments. And that is something all of us should aspire to.

CRAZY MIRRORS

Mirrors come in all sizes and shapes. Sometimes it's a prophet who helps us see the blind spots in our lives. Sometimes it's an epiphany that pulls back the veil and reveals the glory of God in new ways. But the greatest mirror, the mirror that gives us the truest reflection of ourselves, is Scripture.

The best form of self-examination is simply reading Scripture. Or maybe I should say, meditating on Scripture. After all, the Bible wasn't meant to be read. It was meant to be meditated upon. And Psalm 51 is the quintessential example. You can't just read it with your mind. You've got to feel it with your heart. And the way you feel it is by putting yourself in David's sandals. The best way to identify with his guilt is by identifying your own guilt. Some truths can't be accessed by left-brain logic. They are only unlocked in your heart of hearts. And that requires more than a glance in the mirror. Just as you study yourself in the mirror before an important date or important meeting (and I know you do), you have to meditate on the reflection you see.

The book of James likens the Bible to a mirror.[8] Meditating on it is the way we can get an accurate picture of who we are. And it not only reveals the sin in our lives. It also reveals the image of God in us. As we meditate on the Bible, the picture of who we are in Christ develops like a Polaroid print.

When I was a kid, our family used to frequent a restaurant called White Fence Farm. There was always a wait, but I didn't mind because the waiting room was like an amusement park. They had games to play. They had a car museum. And there were crazy mirrors, like at carnivals, that would distort your face and figure. I'd spend fifteen minutes contorting myself into every shape imaginable.

In a sense, every mirror is a crazy mirror except Scripture. Scripture is the only perfect mirror because it reveals how our Designer sees us. Most of our identity problems are the result of looking in the wrong mirrors. For many, culture is the only mirror they consult. They allow culture to define them in terms of what is right or wrong, good or bad, acceptable or unacceptable. For others, their primary mirror is the opinion of other people. And those mirrors, no matter how well meaning those people are, will always result in a distorted image. The only perfect mirror is Scripture. And the more you read it, the more you will reflect God. Why? Because the Bible is where God is revealed.

> *We, who with unveiled faces all reflect the Lord's glory, are being transformed into his likeness with ever-increasing glory, which comes from the Lord, who is the Spirit.*[9]

If you want to discover your soulprint, you've got to begin and end with Scripture.

If you aren't reading your Bible as much as you could or should, you'll have identity issues. And let me go out on a limb. If you aren't reading your Bible like you could or should, it's probably because of some sin issue in your life. You don't want to look in the mirror because it's convicting. You'd rather ignore the diagnosis. But if you ignore it, it'll get worse. And the Bible is more than an MRI that reveals what's wrong. It's also the best preventative medicine. It's not only the best cure for identity problems. It's also the best prevention.

GUILTY SECRETS

Nothing is more isolating than secret sin. And the Enemy wants you to keep the secret. Why? Because God will not heal what you do not confess. Confession is the way we accept God's holy diagnosis. And David does that with the help of prophetic confrontation. That confrontation begins a healing process that results in holiness.

Like David, John Donne was considered the greatest poet of his generation. He went to Oxford when he was eleven years old. Then he went on to serve as dean of St. Paul's Cathedral in London. John Donne was successful by every external standard, but he also lived in a state of constant fear because of a secret sin. Before his conversion to Christ, Donne had written obscene poetry to the woman he had secretly married. And that deep, dark secret imprisoned his spirit. He lived in fear that he would be found out.

Many of us are consumed by the same kind of fear. Like Donne, we are imprisoned by a secret sin. But by hiding the truth, we hide from the truth. By hiding our sin, we hide from ourselves. And that instinct is as old as Eden. What was Adam's initial reaction after his original sin? He tried to hide. And we've been hiding ever since. In a sense, the essence of Eden is the freedom to be your naked self. It's having nothing to hide. And so it will be with the Second Eden. Heaven is having nothing to hide. And so is heaven on earth.

Here is a truth the Enemy doesn't want you to discover: keeping sin secret is more spiritually taxing than getting it out in the open. We think we'd die if the truth were discovered, but the truth is, we'd actually come to life.

Let me borrow a scene from Scripture, a familiar one, to picture this.

Lazarus had been dead and in the tomb for four days when Jesus said: "Come out."[10] And oddly enough, Lazarus obeyed.

To fully appreciate this miracle, you have to understand Jewish burial customs. When Lazarus died, his feet would have been bound at the ankles, and his arms would have been tied to his body with linen strips. Then his body would have been wrapped in approximately one hundred pounds of grave clothes. According to some scholars, the head would be wrapped with so many linens that it would measure a foot wide. You get the mental picture. Lazarus was wrapped up like a mummy. Then Jesus said, "Unwrap him and let him go!"

In every Gospel story, there is a picture of the gospel. And this is one of the most visceral. Sin is about so much more than right and wrong. It's about life and death. When we sin, a part of us dies. It's almost like burial clothes are wrapped around us. We are entombed by our own sin and buried alive. Our soul is wrapped up like a mummy. But Jesus is still saying, "Come out." He is still raising the dead. He is still setting the captive free. We come out of death and into life. We come out of sin and into righteousness.

"The glory of God," said Saint Irenaeus, "is a person fully alive." That is why sin grieves the heart of God so deeply. It's not just His justice that is riled. It is also His love that grieves over the little deaths we experience when we sin. But the good news is that God is in the resurrection business. And He doesn't just want to resurrect your body on the day Christ triumphantly returns. He wants to resurrect your personality that has died at the hands of those who have hurt you. He wants to resurrect dreams that have died of disappointment. He wants to resurrect relationships and give them a fresh start. He wants to give you an abundant life, both quantitative and qualitative.

Some people would rather die than confess their sins, but that is exactly what happens when we fail to confess. We die a slow, painful death. But there is another way. And David shows it to us.

HAPPILY FOREVER AFTER

One decision can change your life in dramatic ways. One wrong decision can ruin a reputation you've worked a lifetime to build. One wrong decision can end a marriage or end a career. And almost like David with regard to his fateful walk on the roof deck, many of us look back on a wrong decision with deep regret. We beat ourselves up over a lapse in judgment. We ponder our missteps and wonder, *What if?* We wish we could turn back time and undo what we've done. But we can't. We cannot change the past. But we can learn from it. And that's how we change the future.

I don't know what mistakes you've made. And I can't promise that everyone will forgive and forget. But God will. I can't promise that you will make things right with those you have wronged. After all, they have free will too. But you can make things right with God. The wrong decisions you have made, no matter how devastating they have been to you and to others, don't have to define you. Not if God's grace is still in play. God's grace has a way of turning what seem like final mistakes into single mistakes. And

He'll even redeem those mistakes and turn them into defining moments that help you discover new dimensions of His grace.

This is the worst chapter of David's life. He makes a terrible decision. And it seems like happily ever after is out the window. It seems like his illicit affair and murderous cover-up will result in a tragic ending. But that isn't how David's story ends, is it? And your story doesn't have to end that way either. In fact, it doesn't have to have an ending at all. By virtue of the Resurrection, you can live happily forever after.

All the Old Testament kings are divided into two categories: those who did what was *right* in the eyes of the Lord and those who did what was *wrong* in the eyes of the Lord. David did something wrong, very wrong. But Scripture doesn't classify him in the category of those who did what was wrong.

> *David had done what was right in the eyes of the LORD and had not failed to keep any of the LORD's commands all the days of his life—except in the case of Uriah the Hittite.*[11]

Did you catch the last line? The biblical account doesn't ignore David's sin. It references the greatest mistake of David's life: sleeping with Bathsheba and then killing her husband, Uriah, to attempt a cover-up. But the key word is "except." That sin was an exception to the rule. And your sin can be too. How? Simply by confessing it. When you confess your sin, it no longer defines you.

You are defined by the grace of God. David was counted in the company of kings who did what was *right* in the eyes of the Lord.

David wasn't defined by his sin. And neither are you. Not if you are in Christ. You are no longer defined by what you've done wrong. You are defined by what Christ has done right. His righteousness is your identity. His righteousness is your destiny. And the promise we started with is the promise you need to hang on to: it's never too late to be who you might have been.

Your mistakes may define your past, but they don't have to define your present. And they certainly don't have to define your future. If you're still breathing, it means that God isn't finished with you yet. He is still chipping and chiseling. He is still remodeling you into His image. He is still setting the captive free and creating the unique masterpiece that is you.

The White Stone

For David's sake the LORD his God gave him a lamp in Jerusalem.

—1 KINGS 15:4

When you close your eyes at night, where does your mind take you? What places do you revisit over and over again? What faces reappear in your mind's eye? What scenes are replayed while you're in a REM cycle?

When David closed his eyes at night, he often saw Bathsheba's beautiful silhouette and Goliath's ugly mug. He frequently returned to the Valley of Elah and the Crags of the Wild Goats. But more often than not, David counted sheep—the sheep he used to shepherd, the sheep he knew by name. His mind wandered all the way back to the hillsides on the outskirts of Bethlehem. That's where he learned to shepherd a flock, sling a stone, and play the lyre. In the moments between wakefulness and sleep, David was a shepherd all over again. When he reopened his eyes, he was sleeping on the king's bed, his bed; in the king's palace, his palace. In the time it takes to wake up, the shepherd boy became a king. It was a surreal feeling every time he woke up, because his life felt like a dream. It flooded David's consciousness with a deep sense of gratitude and a deep sense of destiny. And even when his eyes were wide open and David was wide awake, the sense of destiny never dissipated. He never took the dream, his life, for granted. As he looked back on his life, David was awed by God's faithfulness. His life was evidence of God's providence.

> *Then King David went in and sat before the LORD, and he said:*
>
> *"Who am I, O Sovereign LORD, and what is my family, that you have brought me this far? And as if this were not enough in your sight, O Sovereign LORD, you have also spoken about the future of the house of your servant....*
>
> *For the sake of your word and according to your will, you have done this great thing and made it known to your servant.*
>
> *How great you are, O Sovereign LORD! There is no one like you.*[1]

Have you ever had a moment, almost like an out-of-body experience, when you saw yourself in a way you'd never seen yourself before? Someone says something to you or about you that you've never even noticed about yourself. Or you surprise yourself by doing something you didn't know you could do. Or you finally connect the dots between past experiences and present circumstances in a way that reveals the favor of God displayed in your life. This is one of those moments for David. His life flashes before his eyes. And this question is conceived in his mind. It's the question that consumes him: "Who am I, O Sovereign LORD, and what is my family, that you have brought me this far?" David was the last and least member of his family, but he's become the most powerful person in Israel. David was relegated to shepherd duty, but he's now wearing a king's crown. And David can hardly believe who he's become. He can hardly believe how he got here.

The journey of self-discovery begins with the question David asks: *Who am I?* But even more important than the question is *who* the question is directed to. You can direct that question to lots of different people, and you'll get lots of different answers. But there is only One with an omniscient answer.

If David had asked his father, his father would have told him he was a shepherd—nothing more, nothing less. His own father didn't see David's potential. Neither did his brothers. To his brothers, David was nothing more than an errand boy who brought bread to the battlefield. Saul? He said David was "only a boy." And Goliath called him bird food. None of them saw David for who David really was. None of them saw who David could become. But David doesn't direct this question to any of them. He sits before the Lord and he asks Him this question: *Who am I?*

When was the last time you sat in the presence of God and asked God that question?

The reason so many of us are strangers to ourselves is because we don't sit before the Lord. If you want to discover your destiny, you've got to spend time in the presence of God. There is no alternative. There is no substitute. True self-discovery happens only in the presence of God. It's only when you seek God that you will find yourself. And if you try to find yourself outside of a relationship with your Designer, it will lead to a case of mistaken identity.

THE FINAL MYSTERY

"The final mystery is oneself," observed Oscar Wilde in his letter *De Profundis.* "When one has weighed the sun in the balance, and measured the steps of the moon, and mapped out the seven heavens star by star, there still remains oneself. Who can calculate the orbit of his own soul?"

It's easy to feel unimportant or insignificant when there are billions of people roaming the planet, but you are invaluable and irreplaceable. Let me put it in familiar and familial terms. If you told me that two out of my three children would love me at the end of their lives, do you think that would be good enough for me? No way! Each of my children is invaluable and irreplaceable. So is their love for me and my love for them. I cherish each of my children uniquely. I don't love my kids equally. No parent does. I love each of them uniquely because each of them is unique. And that's how God loves us: uniquely. He loves each of us as if there were only one of us. Why? Because there *is* only one of us! His love for you is unlike His love for anyone else.

And that brings us all the way back to where we began.

There never has been and never will be anyone like you, but that isn't a testament to you. It's a testament to the God who created you. Your uniqueness isn't just a gift from God. It's your gift to God. It's that uniqueness that enables you to worship God unlike anyone who has ever lived. No one can worship God *like you* or *for you*. And by worship, I mean so much more than singing a few songs on Sunday morning. The best form of worship is becoming the best version of who God has created you to be. Worship is more than a lifestyle. Worship is life.

Self-discovery always leads in one of two directions: self-worship or worship of God. If you don't acknowledge uniqueness as a gift from God, then self-discovery will translate into an over-inflated ego, and pride will short-circuit everything God wants to do in you and through you. That's when self-help can become self-destructive. If, however, you see your uniqueness as a gift from God to be stewarded, then it leads to a life of worship. Your uniqueness reveals God's greatness. And that is precisely what David declares. He doesn't celebrate himself. He celebrates God: "Therefore you are great, O LORD God."[2]

THE WHITE STONE

The soulprint is the truest reflection of God's image. Locked within its vaults are your true identity and true destiny. And part of what makes it mysterious is that it's so multidimensional. It contains past, present, and future. It's who I was, who I am, and who I am becoming. Frederick Buechner describes it this way:

> *Beneath the face I am a family plot. All the people I have ever been are buried there—the bouncing boy, his mother's*

pride; the pimply boy and secret sensualist; the reluctant infantryman; the beholder at dawn through hospital plate-glass of his first-born child. All these selves I was I am no longer, not even the bodies they wore are my body any longer, and although when I try, I can remember scraps and pieces about them, I can no longer remember what it felt like to live inside their skin. Yet they live inside my skin to this day, they are buried in me somewhere, ghosts that certain songs, tastes, smells, sights, tricks of weather can raise, and although I am not the same as they, I am not different either because their having been then is responsible for my being now.

Buechner also adds this caveat: "Buried in me too are all the people I have not been yet but might be someday."[3] And that includes who we will be in eternity. As long as we are clothed in flesh, we're unable to see the majesty and mystery of who we truly are. But it will one day be revealed.

A day is coming when we will hear the voice of God, and He will call us by a name unknown to anyone else but Him. It will be a name we've never heard, but we will know it's our name. It's a name we were given before our birth, but it's a name that will be revealed only after our death. That name, our true name, will reveal who we really are.

He who has an ear, let him hear what the Spirit says to the churches. To him who overcomes, I will give some of the

hidden manna. I will also give him a white stone with
a new name written on it, known only to him who
receives it.[4]

It's not the number of breaths we take that makes life worth living. It's the number of things that take our breath away. In those breathless moments, our souls are inflated with awe. It's like heaven invades earth and time stands still. One of my most recent breathless moments was getting my first glimpse of the Grand Canyon. My son Parker and I walked into the Grand Canyon Lodge on the North Rim, and the view through the two-story picture window stopped us in our tracks. Beauty has a way of stopping the second hand. We stared out that window for what seemed like hours.

I think heaven will consist of countless moments like that one. Our glorified senses will absorb the glory of God in unearthly ways. We will see awe-inspiring sights previously imperceptible to the human eye. We will hear angels' voices in an octave previously imperceptible to the human ear. Even our glorified olfactory bulbs will detect aromas that will make us forget every airport Cinnabon we've ever walked by.

The greatest moment in eternity will be the moment your eyes behold Christ—the One who died for you. But a close second (if these eternal moments can even be ranked) will be hearing your heavenly Father call you by your new name for the first time. It will be a name you've never heard before, but it will be like hearing the name you've been called by your entire life. That name will make your entire life make sense.

All the pain.

All the joy.

All the fears.

All the hopes.

All the confusion.

All the dreams.

In that moment your entire life will make sense because God will reveal who you really are. That new name will capture the true essence of who you are, and it will encompass all that you will become in eternity. Your soulprint will finally be given its true name.

I'm not sure if other parents wrestle with this as much I did, but one of the most difficult things I've ever done is name our children. Lora and I felt tremendous pressure over this, our first official act as parents. And we didn't want to mess our kids up for life by giving them the wrong names. The three names we landed on were Parker, Summer, and Josiah. For what it's worth, lots of people ask us if we got saved between the second and third child because we went with a biblical name for number three. Nope. In case you care, Josiah might have been Jonas, but while Lora was in labor, I had one of those "his name shall be" moments.

Along with naming our children, I've also given them dozens of nicknames over the years. We were actually concerned that Parker might not know his real name because he had so many nicknames. So why do we give nicknames? I think there are several reasons. Different nicknames reveal different dimensions of their personalities. Different nicknames reveal different dimensions of our relationships with them. But most significant, nicknames reveal what we see in them.

When Jesus looked at Simon, he saw Peter. So he called him Rock. When he looked at James and John, he saw Sons of Thunder. Those new names revealed the God-given potential that He saw buried beneath their personalities.

In the same way, God sees you, the true you. He sees who He created you to become. And the unique name He has for each one of us is His way of calling us into our true destinies. I'm not sure how this is possible, but that new name will capture every dimension of who we are. Maybe it'll be a really long name, or maybe it'll be hyphenated. Who knows? But what a moment that will be when we hear our heavenly Father speak our new names for the first time! That white stone will become our most treasured possession because it will reveal who we are in the eyes of our omniscient Creator.

But that isn't where the story ends.

FOR DAVID'S SAKE

Generations had come and gone. David was a distant memory. And the engraving on his tombstone was fading. But David's legacy was still alive and well. More than five decades after the death of David, God established Asa, the son of Abijah, as king of Judah.

But God did not establish Asa in that role because of the righteousness of his father, Abijah. In fact, Abijah did what was wrong in the eyes of the Lord.

> *Nevertheless, for David's sake the LORD his God gave him a lamp in Jerusalem, setting up his son after him, and establishing Jerusalem, because David did what was right in the eyes of the LORD.*[5]

Did you catch it? Why did God establish Asa as king of Judah? It wasn't for his sake. God did it for one reason and one reason alone: "for David's sake."

I'm not sure we can even grasp the profundity of that statement, but the implications are incalculable. Sometimes the blessings we enjoy are not the by-product of anything we've done. Sometimes they are the by-product of someone's faithfulness generations ago. And that person's faithfulness nets blessings decades after he or she has died.

That is certainly true in my life. I had grandparents who prayed for me, and their prayers outlived them. My grandfather was hard of hearing. At night he'd take off his hearing aid, kneel beside his bed, and pray for his grandchildren. He couldn't hear himself, but everybody else in the house could. Some of the most humbling moments of my life have been those moments when the Spirit of God has said to my spirit: *The prayers of your grandparents are being answered in your life right now.* Those are defining moments.

I've come to realize that my destiny is inextricably linked to my parents' and grandparents' legacies. And my legacy will influence the destiny of my children, grandchildren, and great-grandchildren.

Does such a possibility scare you, given what your family has been like? It shouldn't. If you are a child of God, you are part of the family of God. Your destiny is Jesus Christ's legacy. The moment you put your faith in Christ, you begin a new chapter, a chapter that will never end. And you answer to a new name. All the promises of God are yours to claim. And all curses, both generational and spiritual, are broken. Simply put: you don't have to make the same mistakes your parents made. And for the record, Asa didn't. Unlike his dad, but just like his great-great-grandfather David, he did what was right in the eyes of the Lord.

Your destiny is your legacy. You inherit a legacy from your ancestors. It is part of your birthright. And you leave a legacy for your progeny. It is part of the inheritance you leave behind. David served God's purpose in his own generation, but he did more than that. He also left a legacy for generations to come, including the Son of David, Jesus Christ. For what it's worth, that's one of my primary motivations as a writer. It's not just my destiny. It's part of my legacy. For better or for worse, my great-grandchildren will know their great-grandfather because I'm leaving a legacy in written form. But you certainly don't have to write a book to leave a legacy. All you have to do is fulfill your unique destiny. And when you do, your destiny turns into your legacy.

My father-in-law, Bob Schmidgall, pastored Calvary Church in Naperville, Illinois, for more than thirty years. And if I had to epitomize him in one way, it'd be this: he had a huge heart for missions. I've never met anyone more consumed with world missions. And because that is what his life was about, it seemed like that is what his death should be about too. In lieu of flowers, those who attended his funeral were encouraged to give a gift to missions. Then, more than a year after his funeral, our entire family flew to Ethiopia to visit a ten-thousand-member church my father-in-law had helped to establish a few years before. We tearfully presented to the pastor of that church, Betta Mengistu, the monies that had been donated at the funeral. And he tearfully received them. That memory will always rank as one of the defining moments of my life. It dawned on me that long after his death, my father-in-law was still giving to missions! His destiny had become a legacy. And that legacy goes beyond finances.

Our executive pastor and my brother-in-law, Joel Schmidgall, is living out his father's legacy. He got his father's enlarged heart for missions. And he has championed missions at National Community Church. We'll take a dozen missions trips this year. And we dream of the day when we're taking fifty-two trips! Imagine the impact of mission teams coming and going every week of the year. We also gave more than half a million dollars to missions last year. And our vision as a church is not just twenty locations. The driving engine is to be giving two million dollars to missions annually by the year 2020. We don't want to grow more just to grow more. We want to grow more so we can give more. That is our destiny as a church, but it is also our legacy as a family. And that legacy is our destiny.

THE NEXT CHAPTER

The journey of self-discovery reveals more than your destiny. It reveals your legacy. It reveals more than what you remember. It also reveals *how* you will be remembered. And that isn't a passive process. Ultimately, your destiny is determined by your decisions. It's your actions, and reactions, that define you. So don't play the victim. Be the victor. After all, that is who you are in Christ. You are not defined by what you have done wrong. You are redefined by what Christ has done right, His righteousness. And that is both your destiny and His legacy.

There comes a moment in every life when you have the opportunity to step into your destiny. This is that moment. I pray that the last chapter of this book will begin the next chapter in your life. How does it start? By sitting before the Lord and asking this question: *Who am I?* That will jump-start the journey. And that journey of self-discovery will continue throughout all eternity.

Let it begin today.

Discussion
Questions

We are God's masterpiece. He has created us anew in Christ Jesus, so that we can do the good things he planned for us long ago.

—Ephesians 2:10, NLT

have the utmost respect for people willing to do the hard work of figuring out how God made them and where God wants them to go in this life. Discovering your real identity isn't easy. But fulfilling your true destiny makes the journey worth it!

To help you in your own journey of self-discovery, I have created this tool filled with summaries of key ideas from the book and questions that will make you think. Consider the questions on your own if you like. Or better yet, gather some other soulprint archaeologists, and talk through these questions together.

It's thrilling to me to think of what God might show you, and do in you, through your search into how He made you. The potential is infinite. Remember, you are His masterpiece, a one-of-a-kind original, and He isn't done perfecting you yet.

OPENING: SOULPRINT

Too often our true identities get buried beneath the mistakes we've made, the insecurities we've acquired, and the lies we've believed. But we can get back to our true identities and our true destinies—our soulprints—if we're willing to undergo a process of self-discovery. Over time we'll begin to see ourselves as God's masterpieces. We'll see ourselves in His image. And paradoxically, seeing ourselves as conformed to the image of Christ will also mean seeing ourselves as unique. There's no one else like you, no one else like me. And being true to ourselves and true to God enables us to escape regret and find fulfillment.

Questions for Discussion or Reflection

1. Which phrase best describes where you're at on your journey of self-discovery?
   - on the front end, trying to figure out who I am
   - on the back end, trying to remember who I was meant to be
   - somewhere in between, trying to close the gap between who I am and who I want to be

   (optional) *Soulprint* group activity: Share a few pictures of yourself from over the years, and talk about how you've changed on the inside as well as the outside.

*David's defining moment #1: rejecting King Saul's armor and choosing stones for his sling instead. Read 1 Samuel 17 (*key verses:* 38–40).

2. When you think about the choice David had to make—adopt someone else's armor or use his own familiar weapon—what choice does it make you think about in your own life?

3. Do you have a talent that others aren't aware of? An idiosyncrasy? An experience others may not know about? Describe it.

4. When you think about Christ's character, what are some adjectives that come to mind? (Examples: *compassionate, determined.*) Which of these adjectives describe your own character?

5. What did God design you to accomplish in this life? Where are you at in fulfilling that destiny?

SCENE I: HOLY CONFIDENCE

Who likes delays and disappointments? Nobody. But what if we started looking at them as opportunities for our soulprints to be more fully formed in us? God has a way of using perceived disadvantages to refine and redefine us. So we need to stop putting our confidence in the things we think we can control. And we need to start putting our confidence—a holy confidence—in what God is doing, regardless of how painful it may be in the short run. In this way our disappointments become divine appointments and we develop an inner unconquerableness.

Questions for Discussion or Reflection

*David's defining moment #2: using his skills with the harp and the slingshot in new ways. Read 1 Samuel 16–17 (*key verses:* 16:14–23 and 17:34–37).

1. Imagine that you were transported back in time to a hillside near Bethlehem and told the shepherd boy David, "You know, one day you will use your harp to soothe the king, and you will use your slingshot to kill Israel's most fearsome enemy." What do you think he would say in response?

2. Name a compensatory skill that you've developed—something you've learned to do to compensate for a disadvantage. How does this compensatory skill help to reveal your identity and your destiny?

3. Looking back on your past, what is one way that God took a delay, disappointment, or disadvantage and used it for good in your life?

   • How did it cultivate your character? *or...*

   • develop one of your gifts? *or...*

   • teach a lesson you could not have learned any other way?

   (optional) *Soulprint* group activity: Take a sheet of paper and draw a dozen or so dots on it, giving each dot a label that identifies a defining moment (good or bad) in your life. Share your work with others in the group, and talk about what this game of connect the dots reveals about your soulprint.

4. Would you say that you're growing in your ability to trust God in the hard spots of life? If so, how?

5. What perceived disadvantages in your life right now seem to be hindering you? How might God use them to help you fulfill the destiny He has in mind for you?

Scene II: Lifesymbols

The past matters. And so it's important to create memorials to our memories—lifesymbols—to remember the important events that have formed who we are and who we are becoming. God will help us choose what to remember and teach us how to give them the right meaning. Our lifesymbols will then becoming powerful means of connecting our identities with our destinies.

Questions for Discussion or Reflection

1. If it's true that our combination of memories makes us who we are, as this chapter declares, then who are you?

2. Are you the kind of person who tends to think about the past a lot, perhaps observing special anniversaries or using photos as memory aids? Or do you mostly stay focused on the present or the future? Why do you think you are that way?

*David's defining moment #3: killing Goliath and keeping Goliath's armor. Reread 1 Samuel 17 (*key verses:* 51–54).

3. In the months and years that followed his victory over Goliath, what do you think David was reminded of when he looked at the giant's armor?
   (optional) *Soulprint* group activity: Do a show-and-tell with one or more of your most precious keepsakes, explaining why they're meaningful to you.

4. What kind of memory management do you need to do to move toward your God-given destiny? What past events do you need to start recalling to memory? Stop remembering so much? Reinterpret?

5. When you think about your very earliest memories, which one stands out? What do you think Alfred Adler's phrase "And so life is" means when applied to this memory?

6. What tangible symbols or mementos could you use to remind yourself of some of the defining moments in your life?

Scene III: The Crags of the Wild Goats

We tend to think that *what we do* in life is what's most important. But to God, *who we become* is far more important. This means that a big part of our soulprints is a matter of character. We have to have integrity. We can't take shortcuts, because if we do, we'll short-circuit God's plan for our lives. He's given us consciences and willpower to choose what's right. As we obey Him and live with integrity, we may not earn all the praise from the world that we crave, but we'll do what matters more: give glory to God.

Questions for Discussion or Reflection

(optional) *Soulprint* group activity: Have each group member write his or her answer to the question, If you had to describe yourself in one word, what would it be? on a slip of paper. Mix up the slips, then see if the group can guess who wrote which word.

1. How strong would you say is your desire for attention and
   praise from other people?
   • very strong
   • somewhat strong
   • not particularly strong
   Give an example of how your craving for approval from
   other people has threatened your integrity.

*David's defining moment #4: sparing King Saul's life. Read 1
Samuel 24 (*key verses:* 3–7).

2. What ethical principle was David tempted to violate here?
   Why was his integrity in this matter so important?
3. Give an example of how a failure in integrity derailed someone's progress toward the vision God had for his or her life.
4. Have you ever had to make a choice between offending
   people and offending God? If so, describe the situation.
5. What connection do you see between humility and
   integrity?
6. Right now (if you're willing to share it), what is one area
   where you are struggling with your integrity? If you fail, what
   harm might it do? If you succeed, what will be the benefit?

SCENE IV: ALTER EGO

No one likes to be embarrassed. But there's nothing like embarrassment to free us from the burden of pretense. If we want to

know our soulprints, we need to embrace embarrassment. That is, we need to be willing to be stripped of the false things we find our identities in. After all, it's far better to find our identities in Christ than in some image we laboriously build up for the world to see. And that's why we need to accept the awkwardness of doing God's will, for He will in turn clothe our embarrassing spiritual nakedness with His cloak of identity.

Questions for Discussion or Reflection

1. What was one of your more embarrassing moments (that you're willing to share)? As you look back on that experience, what does it show you about how you had been projecting a false image of yourself to others?

*David's defining moment #5: dancing before the ark of the covenant. Read 2 Samuel 6 (*key verses:* 12–16, 20–22).

2. What do you admire in David as you look at this incident in his life?
3. Describe someone you know whose uninhibited joy in the Lord inspires your respect.
4. Most Christians would agree that it's important to "find one's identity in Christ." But how does one actually go about doing that?
5. In what way do you think God might be calling you to accept awkwardness or embarrassment right now? How do you think it will help in your own journey of self-discovery?

(optional) *Soulprint* group activity: Pull out the Wii and play *Dance Dance Revolution*. Or try the electric slide as a group.

SCENE V: THE DEVIL'S WORKSHOP

Another part of discovering our soulprints is coming to grips with our sinfulness. We've got to take a long, hard look in the mirror and admit our sins to ourselves and to God, because only then can He begin to re-lay the foundation of our lives. One important key to this is letting someone else be a prophet to us, telling us what we're really like. An even more important key is letting the Scriptures serve as our mirror, comparing and contrasting our behavior with the commands of God. Then, as we confess our sin, our past mistakes will no longer define us. Christ's righteousness will define us.

Questions for Discussion or Reflection

*David's defining moment #6: staying home from war and sinning with Bathsheba. Read 2 Samuel 11–12 (*key verses:* 11:1–4 and 12:7, 13).

1. Which do you find more remarkable, and why?
   - that David would stoop to adultery and murder
   - that he would immediately and humbly accept the prophet's condemnation
2. Give an example of a time when boredom or idleness led you toward sin.

3. What makes ignoring one's own sin an obstacle to living out one's God-given identity?

4. When has someone acted as a prophet for you, helping you to recognize or admit your own sin? Describe the situation. How do you feel about acting as a prophet in this way for others?

5. Describe a time when Scripture convicted you of wrongdoing.

6. The point of this chapter is that you need not be defined by your sin; you can be defined by Christ's righteousness. How do you need to apply this point in your life today? (optional) *Soulprint* group activity: Take turns reading aloud a verse from Psalm 51 that expresses something you are feeling right now or something you want to say to God.

CLOSING: THE WHITE STONE

The journey of self-discovery begins with asking God, *Who am I?* because true self-discovery happens only in the presence of God. And as we acknowledge our uniqueness as a gift from God, it leads to a life, not of selfish pride, but of worship toward God. One day He will give each of us a name that will capture the true essence of who we are and who we will become in eternity. In the meantime we should recognize that fulfilling our soulprints becomes both our destinies and the legacies we leave to those who come after us.

Questions for Discussion or Reflection

1. What have some of the key people in your life told you about who you are? How might their messages agree with or differ from who God says you are?

2. Have you ever gone to God and asked Him to instruct you in who you really are? If so, what did you learn from it?

3. How are you able to worship God differently from all others (defining "worship" in the broadest possible way as a life that gives God glory)?

*David's defining moment #7: receiving God's promise to establish his house. Read 2 Samuel 7 (*key verses:* 18–21).

4. What do you think David learned in the course of his life about who God made him to be?

5. How have you come to understand your identity better during the reading of *Soulprint*? How have you come to understand your destiny better? What work do you still have cut out for you as you lay claim to your soulprint?

6. What legacy has been left to you by parents or grandparents?

7. If you were to die today, what kind of legacy would you be leaving future generations? In contrast, what kind of legacy would you *like* to leave, and what does that say about how you need to better understand and fulfill your soulprint? (optional) *Soulprint* group activity: Take turns "renaming" each other by identifying Scripture verses you see exemplified in one another's lives.

Notes

Opening: Soulprint

1. Meg Greenfield, *Washington* (New York: PublicAffairs, 2001), 23, 61–62, 76–77, 20.
2. Psalm 139:16.
3. Acts 13:36.
4. Ephesians 2:10, NLT.
5. See Luke 4:18.
6. 1 Samuel 17:38–39.
7. 1 Samuel 17:39.
8. See 1 Samuel 17:38–39.

Scene I: Holy Confidence

1. Malcolm Gladwell, "The Uses of Adversity," *New Yorker,* November 10, 2008, http://www.newyorker.com/reporting/2008/11/10/081110fa_fact_gladwell?currentPage=all
2. 1 Samuel 17:34–37.
3. See 1 Samuel 16:16–21.
4. 1 Samuel 17:37.
5. David McCasland, *Oswald Chambers: Abandoned to God: The Life Story of the Author of "My Utmost for His Highest"* (Grand Rapids: Discovery, 1993), 190.

6. Romans 8:37.

7. Philippians 1:6.

Scene II: Lifesymbols

1 Mitch Albom, *Tuesdays with Morrie* (New York: Random House, 1997) 118, 120–21.

2. W. Penfield, "Memory Mechanisms," *A.M.A. Archives of Neurology and Psychiatry* 67 (1952): 178–98, quoted in Thomas A. Harris, M.D., *I'm OK—You're OK* (1969; repr., New York: Quill, 2004), 5–9

3. George Russell, "Germinal," in *Vale and Other Poems* (New York: Macmillan, 1931), 29.

4. Alexandr Solzhenitsyn, *The Oak and the Calf: Sketches of Literary Life in the Soviet Union* (San Francisco: Harper & Row, 1980), 111.

Scene III: The Crags of the Wild Goats

1. Luke 14:8, NLT.

2. See Luke 22:24.

3. 1 Samuel 24:3–4.

4. 1 Samuel 24:5–7.

5. John 10:18.

6. Matthew 26:53.

7. 1 Samuel 24:11–12, 15, NLT.

8. 1 Samuel 24:17, 19–20, NLT.

9. Daniel 3:27, NLT.

10. 1 Samuel 14:35, NLT.

11. 1 Samuel 15:12, NLT.
12. 1 Samuel 15:17.
13. See 1 Samuel 18:9.

Scene IV: Alter Ego
1. 2 Samuel 6:22.
2. 2 Samuel 6:16, NLT.
3. 2 Samuel 6:20–22.
4. Ezekiel 28:17.
5. See Matthew 7:27.

Scene V: The Devil's Workshop
1. 2 Samuel 11:1–3.
2. Psalm 51:3–5.
3. Frederick Buechner, *The Sacred Journey* (New York: Harper-Collins, 1982), 46.
4. Paraphrase of C. S. Lewis, *Mere Christianity* (1952; repr., New York: HarperCollins, 2001), 205.
5. Psalm 51:8, NLT.
6. Laurie Beth Jones, *The Power of Positive Prophecy: Finding the Hidden Potential in Everyday Life* (New York: Hyperion, 1999), ix.
7. Numbers 11:29.
8. See James 1:23–25.
9. 2 Corinthians 3:18.
10. John 11:1–44, NLT.
11. 1 Kings 15:5.

Closing: The White Stone

1. 2 Samuel 7:18–19, 21–22.
2. 2 Samuel 7:22, ESV.
3. Frederick Buechner, *The Alphabet of Grace* (San Francisco: HarperOne, 1989), 14.
4. Revelation 2:17.
5. 1 Kings 15:4–5, ESV.

1

Two Thousand Stairs

The farther backward you look, the further forward you
are likely to see.

—WINSTON CHURCHILL

We hopped on a double-decker bus and headed toward
the heart of Rome. Lora and I had spent a year planning
the trip, but nothing prepares you to stand in the very place where
Caesars ruled an empire or gladiators battled to the death. As we
walked the Via Sacra, we were stepping on the same two-thousand-
year-old stones that conquering armies marched on. Of course,
I'm guessing they weren't licking gelatos. Our three days in the
Eternal City went by far too fast. And I wish we hadn't waited
until our fifteenth anniversary to take the trip.

Few places on earth are as historic or romantic as Rome. We
thoroughly enjoyed strolling the ancient streets, people-watching
in the piazzas, and eating leisurely meals at sidewalk cafés. And

like good tourists, we also hit all the must-see travel-book destinations. We threw pennies over our shoulders into the Trevi Fountain, enjoyed an unplugged concert by an electric guitarist outside the Colosseum one moonlit evening, and took a three-hour tour of St. Peter's Basilica. And all the sites lived up to their travel-book billing. But one of the unexpected highlights of our trip was an unplanned visit to a rather nondescript church off the beaten path. It wasn't referenced in our travel guides. And if it hadn't been right around the corner from our hotel, we would never have discovered it. The Church of San Clemente was named after the fourth pope, who was martyred for his faith. According to legend, anchors were tied around his ankles and he was thrown into the Black Sea.

From the outside, the church appeared weather-beaten and timeworn. But the frescoes, statues, and altars on the inside were remarkably well preserved. We quietly explored every nook and cranny of that twelfth-century church. Then we discovered that for five extra euros we could take an underground tour. As was the case with many of the ruins we visited in Rome, there were several layers of history in the same place. The Romans had a habit of building things on top of things. Some emperors, for example, would tear down their predecessor's palace and build their own palace right on top of it. Such was the case with the Church of San Clemente. The twelfth-century church was built over a fourth-century church. And beneath the fourth-century church were catacombs where second-century Christians secretly worshiped God before the legalization of Christianity by Constantine in 313.

I'll never forget my descent down that flight of stairs. The air became damp, and we could hear underground springs. We carefully navigated each step as we lost some of our light. And our voices echoed off the low ceiling and narrow walkway. Almost like the wardrobe in the Chronicles of Narnia, that flight of stairs was like a portal to a different time, a different place. It was as if those stairs took us back two thousand years in time. With each step, a layer of history was stripped away until all that was left was Christianity in all its primal glory.

As we navigated those claustrophobic catacombs, I was overcome by the fact that I was standing in a place where my spiritual ancestors risked everything, even their lives, to worship God. And I felt a profound mixture of gratitude and conviction. I live in a first-world country in the twenty-first century. And I'm grateful for the freedoms and blessings I enjoy because of where and when I live. But when you're standing in an ancient catacomb, the comforts you enjoy make you uncomfortable. The things you complain about are convicting. And some of the sacrifices you've made for the cause of Christ might not even qualify under a second-century definition.

As I tried to absorb the significance of where I was, I couldn't help but wonder if our generation has conveniently forgotten how inconvenient it can be to follow in the footsteps of Christ. I couldn't help but wonder if we have diluted the truths of Christianity and settled for superficialities. I couldn't help but wonder if we have accepted a form of Christianity that is more educated but less powerful, more civilized but less compassionate, more acceptable but less authentic than that which our spiritual ancestors practiced.

Over the last two thousand years, Christianity has evolved in lots of ways. We've come out of the catacombs and built majestic cathedrals with all the bells and steeples. Theologians have given us creeds and canons. Churches have added pews and pulpits, hymnals and organs, committees and liturgies. And the IRS has given us 501(c)(3) status. And there is nothing inherently wrong with any of those things. But none of those things is primal. And I wonder, almost like the Roman effect of building things on top of things, if the accumulated layers of Christian traditions and institutions have unintentionally obscured what lies beneath.

I'm not suggesting that we categorically dismiss all those evolutions as unbiblical. Most of them are simply abiblical. There aren't precedents for them in Scripture, but they don't contradict biblical principles either. I'm certainly not demonizing postmodern forms of worship. After all, the truth must be reincarnated in every culture in every generation. And I am personally driven by the conviction that there are ways of doing church that no one has thought of yet. But two thousand years of history raises this question: when all of the superficialities are stripped away, what is the primal essence of Christianity?

In the pages that follow, I want you to descend that flight of stairs with me. I want us to go underground. I want us to go back in time. Think of it as a quest for the lost soul of Christianity. And by the time you reach the last page, I hope you will have done more than rediscover Christianity in its most primal form. I hope you will have gone back to the primal faith *you* once had. Or more accurately, the primal faith that once had you.

THE FAR SIDE OF COMPLEXITY

My kids are at that stage in their mathematical journey where they are learning about prime numbers. That means that, as a parent, I am relearning about prime numbers (along with every other math concept I have long since forgotten). A prime number is a number that is divisible only by itself and the number 1. And while an infinitude of prime numbers exists, the only even prime is the number 2.

Certain truths qualify as prime truths. Bible-believing, God-fearing, Christ-loving Christians will disagree about a variety of doctrinal issues until Jesus returns, whether that be pre-, mid-, or post-Tribulation. That is why we have hundreds of different denominations. But prime truths have an indivisible quality to them. And chief among them—the even prime, if you will—is what Jesus called the most important commandment. We call it the Great Commandment. It could also be called the Primal Commandment because it is of first importance.

Love the Lord your God with all your heart and with all your soul and with all your mind and with all your strength.

Jesus was a genius. He had the ability to simplify complex spiritual truths in unforgettable and irrefutable ways. I'm afraid we tend to do the opposite. We complicate Christianity. That religious tendency to overcomplicate simple spiritual truths traces all the way back to a sect of Judaism known as the Pharisees. Over the span of hundreds of years, the Pharisees compiled a comprehensive list of religious dos and don'ts. Six hundred and thirteen, to be exact. Jesus peeled them back with one primal statement. When all of the rules and regulations, all of the traditions and institutions, all of the liturgies and methodologies are peeled back, what's left is the Great Commandment. It is Christianity in its most primal form.

Sounds so simple, doesn't it? If only it were as simple as it sounds.

Oliver Wendell Holmes, former chief justice of the Supreme Court, once made a perceptive distinction between two kinds of simplicity: simplicity on the near side of complexity and simplicity on the far side of complexity. He said, "I would not give a fig for simplicity on the near side of complexity."

Many Christians settle for simplicity on the near side of complexity. Their faith is only mind deep. They know *what* they believe, but they don't know *why* they believe what they believe. Their faith is fragile because it has never been tested intellectually or experientially. Near-side Christians have never been in the catacombs of doubt or suffering, so when they encounter questions they cannot answer or experiences they cannot explain, it causes a crisis of faith. For far-side Christians, those who have done their time in the catacombs of doubt or suffering, unanswerable questions and unexplainable experiences actually result in a heightened appreciation for the mystery and majesty of a God who does not fit within the logical constraints of the left brain. Near-side

Christians, on the other hand, lose their faith before they've really found it.

Simplicity on the near side of complexity goes by another name: *spiritual immaturity*. And that's not the kind of simplicity I'm advocating. God calls us to simplicity on the far side of complexity. For that matter, He calls us to faith on the far side of doubt, joy on the far side of sorrow, and love on the far side of anger. So how do we get there? Well, there are no easy answers or quick fixes. It involves unlearning and relearning everything we know. It involves deconstructing and reconstructing everything we do. It involves the painstaking process of rediscovering and reimagining the primal essence of Christianity. But the result is simplicity on the far side of complexity. And that is where this flight of stairs will take us if we have the courage to go underground.

THE PRIMAL PROBLEM

It goes without saying that Christianity has a perception problem. At the heart of the problem is the simple fact that Christians are more known for what we're *against* than what we're *for*. But the real problem isn't perception. We as Christians are often quick to point out what's wrong with our culture. And we certainly need the moral courage to stand up for what's right in the face of what's wrong. I live in the bastion of political correctness, where it is wrong to say that something is wrong. And that's wrong. If we have to choose between political correctness and biblical correctness, we must choose biblical correctness every time. But before confronting what's wrong with our culture, we need to be humble enough, honest enough, and courageous enough to repent of what's wrong with us.

I pastor a church in Washington DC that is nearly 70 percent single twenty-somethings. Unfortunately, our demographics are an anomaly. By and large, twenty-somethings are leaving the church at an alarming rate. According to some statistics, 61 percent of twenty-somethings who grew up going to church will quit going to church in their twenties. And the temptation is to ask this question: what's wrong with this generation? But that is the wrong question. The right question is this: what's wrong with the church?

My answer is simply this: we're not great at the Great Commandment. In too many instances, we're not even good at it.

That, I believe, is our primal problem. That is the lost soul of Christianity. If Jesus said that loving God with all our heart, soul, mind, and strength is the most important commandment, then doesn't it logically follow that we ought to spend an inordinate amount of our time and energy trying to understand it and obey it? We can't afford to be merely good at the Great Commandment. We've got to be great at the Great Commandment.

The quest for the lost soul of Christianity begins with rediscovering what it means to love God with all our heart, soul, mind, and strength. Jesus used those four kaleidoscopic words to describe four dimensions of love. And there is certainly overlap among them. It's hard to know where loving God with your heart ends and loving God with your soul begins. But one thing is sure: loving God in one way isn't enough. It's not enough to love God with *just* your heart or soul or mind or strength. We are called, even commanded, to love Him in all four ways. Think of it as love to the fourth power.

So the quest begins with rediscovery. But it ends with reimagination. Some truths can be deduced via left-brain logic. Others are better induced via right-brain imagination. Love falls into the latter category. So what follows is not a strict exposition of the Great Commandment. It's a reimagination of the four primal elements detailed by Jesus in the Great Commandment:

The heart of Christianity is primal compassion.
The soul of Christianity is primal wonder.
The mind of Christianity is primal curiosity.
And the strength of Christianity is primal energy.

The descent down this flight of stairs into primal Christianity will be convicting at points, but the end result will be a renewed love for God that is full of genuine compassion, infinite wonder, insatiable curiosity, and boundless energy. Anything less is not enough. It's not just unfulfilling, it's also unfaithful. The quest is not complete until it results in catacomb-like convictions that go beyond conventional logic. The goal is a love that, as our spiritual ancestors understood, is worth living for and dying for.

THE WAY FORWARD

My aim in this book is to take you to new places intellectually and spiritually so that you discover new ways of loving God. But I also hope this book takes you back to a primal place where God loved you and you loved God. And that's all that mattered.

I've discovered that when I've lost my way spiritually, the way forward is often backward. That is what we experience when we celebrate Communion, isn't it? Communion is a pilgrimage back to the foot of the cross. And going back to that most primal place helps us find our way forward. So before going forward, let me encourage you to go backward. Go back to that place where God opened your eyes and broke your heart with compassion for others. Go back to that place where the glory of God flooded your soul and left you speechless with wonder. Go back to that place where thoughts about God filled your mind with holy curiosity. Go back to that place where a God-given dream caused a rush of adrenaline that filled you with supernatural energy.

Every year our entire church staff goes on a pilgrimage to the Catalyst Conference in Atlanta, Georgia. During one of the sessions this past year, our team was sitting in the balcony of the Gwinnett Center listening to my friend and the pastor of Life Church.tv, Craig Groeschel. And he asked this question: "Does your heart break for the things that break the heart of God?"

I felt a tremendous sense of conviction when Craig asked that question. As I sat in that balcony, surrounded by twelve thousand other leaders, I heard the still, small voice of the Holy Spirit. The Spirit said to my spirit in His kind yet convicting voice, *Mark, what happened to the college kid who used to pace the chapel balcony seeking My face?*

There are few things I *hate more or appreciate more* than the conviction of the Holy Spirit. It is so painful. But it is so necessary. And I'm so grateful that God loves me enough to break me where I need to be broken. Can I make an observation? You cannot listen to just half of what the Holy Spirit has to say. It's a package deal. If you aren't willing to listen to everything He has to say, you won't hear anything He has to say. If you tune out His convicting voice, you won't hear His comforting voice or guiding voice either. As I was seated in that balcony, the Holy Spirit reminded me of the raw spiritual intensity I once had. He revealed how calloused my heart had become. And I realized that I had somehow lost my soul while serving God. And it wrecked me.

Does your heart break for the things that break the heart of God?

If it doesn't, you need to repent. And that's what I did that day. Our team is typically the first to hit the exit after the last session at conferences because, quite frankly, the first one to the restaurant wins. And we had reservations at one of my favorite restaurants, P.F. Chang's. Love their lettuce wraps and spare ribs. I could almost taste them. But we couldn't leave until we brought closure to what God was doing in the depths of our souls. So we delayed our reservation, found a conference room, and spent some time crying, confessing, and praying as a team. I think we were the last ones to leave the auditorium.

In the providence of God, I happened to be scheduled to speak at my alma mater in Springfield, Missouri, the next week. So a few days later I found myself in the chapel balcony where I had logged hundreds of hours pacing back and forth seeking God.

It was during prayer times in that balcony when my heart began to break for the things that break the heart of God. It was there that God began to shape my soul to seek Him. It was there that God began to fill my mind with God ideas. It was in that balcony that God energized me by giving me a God-sized vision for my life.

Returning to that chapel balcony fifteen years later, I realized that in many ways I had become a paid professional Christian. My heart didn't beat as strongly as it once did. My pulse didn't quicken in the presence of God like it once had. So God took me back to a very primal place. And the Holy Spirit lovingly reminded me that the college kid with a huge heart for God was still somewhere inside me. I knew that getting back what I once had meant getting back to basics. It meant doing what I had once done. It meant rediscovering and reimagining what it means to love God with all my heart, soul, mind, and strength. And somewhere along the way, in my personal quest for my lost soul, I found it. Climbing those stairs into that chapel balcony was like descending those stairs into that ancient catacomb. God gave me back the compassion, wonder, curiosity, and energy I once had, along with an even greater appreciation for what I had lost and found.

Is there a personal catacomb somewhere in your past? A place where you met God and God met you? A place where your heart broke with compassion? A place where your soul was filled with wonder? A place where your mind was filled with holy curiosity? A place where you were energized by a God-ordained dream? Maybe it was a sermon that became more than a sermon. God birthed something supernatural in your spirit. Maybe it was a mission trip or retreat. And you swore you'd never be the same again. Or maybe it was a dream or a vow or a decision you made at an altar. My prayer is that this book will take you down two thousand stairs back to that primal place—the place where loving God with all your heart, soul, mind, and strength is all that matters.

The quest for the lost soul of Christianity begins there.